D0884273

MARGARET MORGAN
and
MARY MORGAN DIXON
Memorial

RIVERSIDE · PUBLIC · LIBRARY

people
in the NEWS

Nicki Minaj

Nicki Minaj

By: Christie Brewer Boyd

LUCENT BOOKS
A part of Gale, Cengage Learning

GALE
CENGAGE Learning·

Detroit • New York • San Francisco • New Haven, Conn • Waterville, Maine • London

© 2013 Gale, Cengage Learning

ALL RIGHTS RESERVED. No part of this work covered by the copyright herein may be repro-
duced, transmitted, stored, or used in any form or by any means graphic, electronic, or
mechanical, including but not limited to photocopying, recording, scanning, digitizing, taping,
Web distribution, information networks, or information storage and retrieval systems, except
as permitted under Section 107 or 108 of the 1976 United States Copyright Act, without the
prior written permission of the publisher.

Every effort has been made to trace the owners of copyrighted material.

Library of Congress Cataloging-in-Publication Data

Boyd, Christie Brewer.
    Nicki Minaj / by Christie Brewer Boyd.
        p. cm. -- (People in the news)
    Includes bibliographical references and index.
    ISBN 978-1-4205-0888-8 (hardcover)
1. Minaj, Nicki--Juvenile literature. 2. Rap musicians--United States--Biography--
Juvenile literature. I. Title.
    ML3930.M64B69 2013
    782.421649092--dc23
    [B]

2012028635

Lucent Books
27500 Drake Rd
Farmington Hills MI 48331

ISBN-13: 978-1-4205-0888-8
ISBN-10: 1-4205-0888-1

Printed in the United States of America
1 2 3 4 5 6 7 16 15 14 13 12

Contents

Fame and celebrity are alluring. People are drawn to those who walk in fame's spotlight, whether they are known for great accomplishments or for notorious deeds. The lives of the famous pique public interest and attract attention, perhaps because their experiences seem in some ways so different from, yet in other ways so similar to, our own.

Newspapers, magazines, and television regularly capitalize on this fascination with celebrity by running profiles of famous people. For example, television programs such as *Entertainment Tonight* devote all their programming to stories about entertainment and entertainers. Magazines such as *People* fill their pages with stories of the private lives of famous people. Even newspapers, newsmagazines, and television news frequently delve into the lives of well-known personalities. Despite the number of articles and programs, few provide more than a superficial glimpse at their subjects.

Lucent's People in the News series offers young readers a deeper look into the lives of today's newsmakers, the influences that have shaped them, and the impact they have had in their fields of endeavor and on other people's lives. The subjects of the series hail from many disciplines and walks of life. They include authors, musicians, athletes, political leaders, entertainers, entrepreneurs, and others who have made a mark on modern life and who, in many cases, will continue to do so for years to come.

These biographies are more than factual chronicles. Each book emphasizes the contributions, accomplishments, or deeds that have brought fame or notoriety to the individual and shows how that person has influenced modern life. Authors portray their subjects in a realistic, unsentimental light. For example, Bill Gates—cofounder of the software giant Microsoft—has been instrumental in making personal computers the most vital tool of the modern age. Few dispute his business savvy, his perseverance, or his technical expertise, yet critics say he is ruthless in his dealings with competitors and driven more by his desire to maintain Microsoft's dominance in the computer industry than by an interest in furthering technology.

In these books, young readers will encounter inspiring stories about real people who achieved success despite enormous obstacles. Oprah Winfrey—one of the most powerful, most watched, and wealthiest women in television history—spent the first six years of her life in the care of her grandparents while her unwed mother sought work and a better life elsewhere. Her adolescence was colored by pregnancy at age fourteen, rape, and sexual abuse.

Each author documents and supports his or her work with an array of primary and secondary source quotations taken from diaries, letters, speeches, and interviews. All quotes are footnoted to show readers exactly how and where biographers derive their information and provide guidance for further research. The quotations enliven the text by giving readers eyewitness views of the life and accomplishments of each person covered in the People in the News series.

In addition, each book in the series includes photographs, annotated bibliographies, timelines, and comprehensive indexes. For both the casual reader and the student researcher, the People in the News series offers insight into the lives of today's newsmakers—people who shape the way we live, work, and play in the modern age.

The Queen of Hip-Hop

Nicki Minaj is a slew of personalities and musical styles crammed into a small package. On the one hand she is a foul-mouthed, fast-spitting rapper prone to switching accents and dropping creative, funny lyrics. On the other hand, she is a megawatt pop star, topping the mainstream charts with danceable songs.

Minaj is just as likely to wear chic outfits and attend Fashion Week as she is to don absurd costumes, making herself into such disparate characters as a robot, a Catholic clergyman, or, most frequently, her vision of a Barbie doll, swathed in what she calls "Harajuku" style. Her fans are equally as diverse, including both hard-core rap fans and eight-year-olds who love to bop along to the newest Top 40 hits. For these reasons, Minaj has been lauded as the first lady of rap, though she has made clear her ambitions hardly stop with conquering just one genre of music.

The New Queen

Like many female emcees before her, Minaj broke onto the scene in large part because of her association with a male hip-hop posse. Minaj's career took off when rapper Lil Wayne brought her into the fold of his record company, Young Money Entertainment. Minaj, however, quickly carved out a reputation for herself as an individual, not cut from the same cloth as the female emcees before her. Minaj realized early that she would need to make music on her own terms in order to create a lasting career. She noted that

Minaj entered the hip-hop scene determined to make a lasting impression in a genre where the careers of female artists are few and fleeting.

none of the prominent female rappers of her adolescence (Lil' Kim, Lauryn Hill, or Eve, for example) had created lasting careers like their male counterparts. She became determined that their fate would not be her own.

The result was that Minaj quickly became a recognized force within the hip-hop community. Before she had put out an original song of her own, music critics and mainstream news sources were taking note of the female rapper that seemed to be spotlighted in everyone else's music. Other artists, too, were singing her praises. After Minaj collaborated with Kanye West on the song "Monster," for example, he applauded her talent and described her as "the scariest artist in the game right now."[1] *Rolling Stone* magazine titled a 2010 profile of Minaj "The New Queen of Hip-Hop," and several other articles lauded her as the revival of the female rapper.

Part of Minaj's buzz had to do with her being the *only* female voice heard rapping at the time—she filled a true void in the industry. In fact, after presenting the female rap solo performance Grammy Award in 2003 and 2004, the Recording Academy (which gives the awards) eliminated the award due to a lack of competitors in the category. When Minaj arrived on the scene in 2008, none of the most recent reigning queens of rap, such as Queen Latifah, Lil' Kim, and Lauryn Hill, had produced a chart-topping hit in several years.

In addition to being the sole female voice among rappers at the beginning of her career, Minaj also had a singular, inimitable style. Mesfin Fekadu, a music critic, wrote, "In the past few years, women rappers were mere blips on the screen, and the occasional hit only underscored how weak the field had become. Until now. Nicki Minaj, the in-your-face, highly animated sex kitten and protégé of rap prince Lil Wayne, has not only emerged as hip-hop's leading female, she's outdoing her male counterparts, too."[2] The CEO of Cash Money Records, the parent company to Lil Wayne's Young Money Entertainment, Bryan "Baby" Williams, went further. He observed that early in her career, Minaj had already become more dominant in the field of rappers than any of the past female emcees had become during their whole careers. Williams said, "The females haven't been as dominant as she's been right now. … We need more of that. [But] she's different from any other female that has done it. She exercises her own vision. It's been magical watching her develop."[3]

As Minaj developed, she dominated not just as a woman but in the entire genre of rap. In early 2012 MTV named her to its annual "Hottest MC" list, a top-ten register of the best MCs (that is, microphone controllers or emcees, otherwise known as rappers) in the game. At number four, she bested her own mentor, Lil Wayne, by one place and became the first female ever to be named to the list without an accompanying male emcee.

"A Purist's Nightmare"

One of the many ways Minaj set herself apart was to diversify her image and sound. She purposefully created music that was outside of the hip-hop mold. While she remained rooted in rap, it was no longer the only genre that could claim her. Minaj successfully experimented with pop and rhythm-and-blues (R&B) sounds, and before she knew it, was a successful pop star. In reviewing her sophomore album, *Pink Friday: Roman Reloaded*, music critic Jody Rosen called Minaj "a purist's nightmare." She explained that Minaj does not merely cross over into multiple genres of pop music; rather, she "dumps them in a Cuisinart, whips them to a frothy purée, then trains a guided missile at the whole mess."[4]

In addition to her skills as a musical performer, Minaj has also become known for her often outrageous appearance. She embraces her role as a starlet, making her looks an inseparable part of her appeal. David Wallace-Wells of *New York* magazine explains that Minaj is unique in her role as a pinup girl for hip-hop, one who cemented her fame "just as much, and maybe more, with her strut, her swag, and her loudmouth-in-outer-space style as by what she sounds like or what she says."[5]

By being a female emcee with street credibility and an artist with an image and crossover sound that appeals to all of America, Minaj has opened doors that have been closed to other leading ladies of hip-hop. She has charted successes not only on the rap and hip-hop charts, where her songs are constantly found, but also on the charts measuring the most popular among *all* songs. Minaj appeals to a strangely wide array of fans—rap fans, R&B and pop fans, forty-year-olds, and elementary-aged kids included. Minaj is turning her rap success into an enduring musical career. She has become the Queen of Hip-Hop, but it is clear Minaj is also making a play for a much bigger title. Indeed, Minaj plans to dominate the entire music industry—for a long time to come.

Chapter 1

Praying for Fame

Nicki Minaj was born Onika Tanya Maraj on December 8, 1982, in Saint James, Trinidad, to parents Omar and Carol Maraj. Though born Onika, her family always called her Nicki. Nicki was born into a large family. Though her immediate family included just her parents and one older brother, during her young life she was often surrounded by numerous cousins, aunts, uncles, and her grandmother.

White Picket Fence

When Nicki was just a toddler, her parents left Trinidad and went to the United States. Nicki and her older brother were left behind with their grandmother in Trinidad. "A lot of times when you're from the islands, your parents will leave and then send for you. Because it's easier when they've established themselves, when they have a place to stay, when they have a job," explains the rap star, who thought she would be in her grandmother's care for just a few days. "It turned into two years without my mother."[6] While her parents got settled in Queens—a borough of New York City just outside of Manhattan—Nicki and her brother lived with her grandmother in a crowded house filled with cousins, aunts, and uncles until Nicki was five years old.

From the suburban town of Saint James on the coast of Trinidad, Nicki imagined what her parents' life was like in New York. Partly because her family did not have much money, Nicki was certain her parents were making a better life in the United States. She thought her parents were spending so much time away because they were busy setting up a lavish life. She imagined in the United States her family would be rich, because as a child she believed everyone in America was rich.

When their mother finally moved Nicki and her brother to Queens, however, Nicki found a very different reality than she had dreamed about. She remembers:

(When I went to New York) I thought it was gonna be like a castle. Like, you know, white picket fence, like a fairy tale … I remember the house. I remember that the furniture wasn't put down. The furniture was, like, piled up on each other, and I didn't understand why, 'cause I thought it was gonna look like a big castle. I started hearing a lot of arguing and I didn't know why. I was always very nervous, very afraid, so I knew that wasn't normal.[7]

Trinidad and Tobago

The Republic of Trinidad and Tobago is a country made up of two large islands and many small ones in the South Caribbean, just north of Venezuela. The country's official language is English, though many of its people speak one of two Creole languages that are based on English. Nicki Minaj's family is from the town of Saint James, a suburb of Port of Spain, the capital city. Port of Spain is located on the northwestern coastline of the larger island, Trinidad.

The ethnic background of the population of Trinidad and Tobago tends to be mixed—a reflection of the centuries of immigration and conquest in the Caribbean. Most of the population of the island nation is a mixture of native Trinidadian and Tobagonian combined with various other nationalities, including African, British, Chinese, Dutch, French, and Indian. Nicki Minaj and her family are of African, Trinidadian, and Indo-Asian descent.

Nicki's parents lived in cramped quarters in Jamaica, Queens. They lived in a small house with fifteen other people and had difficulty making ends meet. Nicki's mother worked hard as a nursing assistant, a steady but low-paying job. Her father, however, became addicted to drugs and alcohol upon moving to Queens. Not only did he contribute very little to the family's finances, he even stole from them on numerous occasions. "We didn't know but he fell victim to crack shortly after he moved to America," said Nicki. "And, when you're on crack, you can't keep a job. And when you can't keep a job, you don't have money. And when you don't have money, you steal. And, you steal from your family. You steal from your wife's pocketbook, and you steal from, you know, you steal your son's video game."[8]

Her father's addiction and the family's financial instability forced them to move constantly. Nicki attended four or five elementary schools in New York City. "We would move all the time," says Nicki, "and whenever we pulled up to a house, I was all hoping, you know, that this was the one, the one with the white picket fence. They were nothing like that."[9]

"I Was Afraid, Very Afraid"

In addition to his drug use, Omar's demeanor was nothing like Nicki remembered from their time together in Trinidad. He frequently yelled and started arguments with other family members. Soon her father exhibited a violent streak, especially toward his wife. Nicki grew up amidst constant arguing and screaming and had nightmares because of her father's violent outbursts. She also began to develop a very deep-seated fear as a young child: "I was afraid, very afraid, that something would happen to my mother,"[10] she recalls.

Though Carol could not temper Omar's moods and anger, she worked hard to provide for her kids. "My mother … kept us together," says Nicki. "She made ends meet. She always kept a job. She always kept her head held high even when she was really, really embarrassed."[11] Carol tried to stand up to Omar, and she threw him out of the house several times. However, Nicki's father would torment the entire family, crying, begging, and stalking them until her mother finally took him back. One time, Nicki remembers

Minaj recalls fearing for her mother's safety as a child when she witnessed her father's quick temper and violent outbursts.

being in the car with her mother when her father unexpectedly pulled Carol from the car. He dragged her several blocks. Nicki became obsessed with locking doors after this, feeling like it was the only thing she could do to protect her mother.

Another time, Omar set fire to the family home while Nicki and her brother were away, but her mother managed to escape the house before she was seriously injured. Although Nicki was terrified for her mother's safety, she credits these terrible experiences with turning her into the strong woman she is today. She also believes these experiences are at the root of her commitment to girl power. "I wanted my mother to be stronger, and she couldn't be,"[12] she explains.

Everything in Nicki's life became overshadowed by fear of her father and the fear that he would take her mother, her only support, away from her. Nicki began to dream up ways she might protect her mother or remove her from the abusive relationship. Nicki prayed every day that she would be able lift her mother from the struggle of her life. She remembers "kneeling at the foot of my mother's bed every morning, saying, 'Please, God, make me rich and famous so that I can take care of her.'"[13]

Nicki grew up watching soap operas with her grandmother in Trinidad and thought that acting might be a track to stardom—and money. She wanted to earn lots of money so that she could take her mother and brother away somewhere that her father would not find them. For Nicki this goal became more than a child's dream; she began to believe with her whole being that becoming rich would solve her family's problems. She began to think she was not like other people, but was instead destined to become famous.

Fantasy Is Reality

Performing and adopting different characters came naturally to young Nicki, making it easy for her to imagine herself as a future actress. From an early age, she loved to sing and act for others, and she would jump up to perform in front of anyone she met. Nicki perfected some of her skills at home. For example, she and her mother liked to talk in different accents while working in the kitchen. Carol would encourage her daughter by asking her to speak in particular accents, especially the ones she could not do herself. Nicki would watch movies with her mother and imitate the various accents she heard until she had mastered them. "I took a special liking to British accents,"[14] she says.

Minaj traces her preferences for colorful hairstyles and unusual outfits to her childhood, when she created new looks and identities a way of escaping her real-life troubles.

Nicki also became interested in changing her look. She started experimenting with her hair when she was nine years old, putting in gels, cornrows, or permanent waves. When she was fourteen, she went to a hair salon and asked for blonde highlights, but the beautician refused because Nicki did not have her mother's permission. Nicki viewed changing her hair around as a way to reinvent herself. She remembers showing off a new hairstyle to her neighbor, who questioned the young girl's style change.

When her neighbor asked why she had changed her hair, Nicki responded, "I'm someone new in this hair."[15]

For Nicki, fantasizing about becoming someone new helped her emotionally escape the violence and poverty of her life. She even created characters that she slipped into in order to keep her mind off of particularly rough times. "'Cookie' was my first identity—that stayed with me for a while," she remembers. "Fantasy was my reality."[16]

The *Fame* School

Nicki's tendency toward theatrics—creating characters, changing her accent, playing with her hair—found an outlet at school. Her fifth-grade teacher staged class plays, which gave Nicki her first taste of real acting. She next joined the school choir at age twelve. When she was ready for high school, Nicki decided to audition for the LaGuardia High School of Music & Art, a prestigious,

Minaj's talent as both a theatrical performer and a singer landed her a spot at the prestigious LaGuardia High School of Music & Art.

specialized public high school in New York City that requires auditions to be admitted. The school has churned out many successful actors, musicians, and dancers, and it was the basis for the hit Broadway musical, movie, and television series *Fame*. The school's aim is to provide each student with professional training in different art forms, all the while giving them an academic background that will prepare them for college. Nicki secured both an acting and a singing audition. However, the day of auditions, her voice was hoarse.

Nicki's Musical Influences

Though Nicki eventually devoted herself to rap, she grew up listening to and loving a wide variety of genres. When she was a child, she heard her mother playing R&B albums by Luther Vandross, Babyface, and Diana Ross. Nicki's first memories of being inspired by an artist were of watching pop star Cyndi Lauper perform on television. Nicki was also inspired by Madonna, Janet Jackson, Grace Jones, and Marilyn Monroe. In her adolescence Nicki embraced the popular female emcees of the day, such as Foxy Brown, Lil' Kim, and Missy Elliott. In her high school yearbook, she had a quote from

Minaj performs with one of her influences, Madonna, at Super Bowl XLVI in 2012.

Lauryn Hill printed below her senior photo. She says she continues to love good music from any genre.

Nicki's singing audition was scheduled first. She went through with the audition, but with her hoarse voice, did not do well. She was so upset that she almost left the school without even auditioning for the acting program. "I failed miserably," she recalls. "I was defeated. I said, 'Forget this school. This stupid school. I don't want to be here anyway. Get me outta here.'"[17] Her mother, however, convinced her to stay and follow through with the acting audition. From the moment the audition began, Nicki knew she was in the right place. "I felt right at home," she says. "I knew this was what I wanted to do for the next 4 years."[18]

Anxious to Grow Up

Nicki was admitted to the drama program at LaGuardia. For the next four years of high school, she took typical high school classes as well as intense acting instruction. She studied acting technique, voice and diction, the history of theater, and dance and body movement. During her senior year, like every other drama student, Nicki also learned how to audition properly. She had the chance to perform in front of real acting agents, who often handed out callback slips to actors and actresses with whom they were interested in working.

Nicki earned the notice of many agents who visited LaGuardia to watch the students perform. She explains, "All the agents come in and you perform and usually you get two or three slips, and that means that that's how many agents are interested in you. I got 10."[19] Although Nicki went on some auditions after she graduated in 2002, she quickly grew impatient with the process. Securing and preparing for auditions could be laborious and time-consuming, and even when hired, work as an actress could be very inconsistent, making it difficult to support oneself. Nicki wanted to be able to support herself as soon as possible—her goal was to get out of her parents' house immediately after high school. She was therefore less interested in going on auditions than she was in finding a job and an apartment of her own.

Hope for a Record Deal

Nicki took several part-time jobs to make ends meet. She worked first as a waitress but was fired from five different jobs, including one at Red Lobster. She worked for a time as a customer service representative and also as an office manager. These and other jobs also ended badly, though; as one writer puts it, at one point "Minaj was getting fired from jobs more often than she was paying her rent on time."[20] Unable to face the prospect of moving

Minaj's motivation to succeed as a rapper was based in her desire to gain fame and riches and be able to support her mother.

back in with her family, she remained dedicated to finding a way to become famous.

Shortly after moving out on her own, a friend in Nicki's neighborhood asked her to write a hook for his rap song. A hook is typically the most memorable thing about a rap or song, usually the chorus or a phrase that is repeated. In addition to writing a compelling chorus, Nicki also provided a verse. Her friend was impressed, and for the first time Nicki realized that rap might be an avenue toward wealth and fame. She began writing more raps, something she had enjoyed doing for fun in high school. She also started to sing backup vocals for underground, unsigned New York rappers. Doing so made for a grueling schedule that kept Nicki working very hard. "That whole time was so horrible," she remembers. "It was like torture."[21] After a long day of working at one of a series of jobs she disliked, she would change her clothes, fix her hair and makeup, and head for the recording studio.

From the moment Nicki set foot in the rap scene in New York, she had one clear goal: to get a record deal. Rapping would be no side hobby for her. She believed rap would be the way she would become famous and rich and that it would give her the means to finally support and protect her mother. Telling her mother she had decided to quit her job and pursue a career as a rapper was not easy, as Nicki explains: "I will never forget the panic and fear in her eyes," she says. "My heart just frickin' collapsed for a second. My mother was always like, 'Yeah, you can do anything,' but her eyes couldn't lie."[22] Despite her mother's trepidation, and despite being uncertain herself whether she could get a record deal, Nicki Minaj was determined to throw herself wholeheartedly into a career as a rap artist.

Chapter 2

Collaboration Queen

Nicki Minaj gave her all to getting herself noticed in New York's underground rap scene. Her dedication paid off, leading her to work with one of the industry greats: Lil Wayne. After moving to Atlanta to be mentored by Lil Wayne, Minaj began to build a reputation by making cameo appearances on other artists' tracks. Before she even released an album of her own, she was being heralded as the woman who would revive female rap, a tall order for an artist new to the scene.

Minaj on Myspace

Like many unsigned musicians in the first few years of the 2000s, Minaj created a Myspace page where fans could hear her music and see photos. Myspace is a social networking site that at the time was very popular, especially for musicians, because the site allowed uploads of MP3s and videos. Unsigned musicians could also sell their music directly through Myspace, helping new musicians to build their audience. Minaj's Myspace page showcased her self-written raps, as well as her provocative promotional photos.

Minaj modeled her earliest rap style after other successful female emcees, such as Lil' Kim and Foxy Brown. Her lyrics were explicitly sexual, as were her promotional photos. She played up her toughness through the use of expletives, sexual boasting, and a fearless bravado in lyrics and gesture. Though Minaj styled herself in the

Before she was signed to a record label, Minaj used MySpace to showcase her early music and build her fan base.

shadows of the stars who had come before her, her original talent and flair for the dramatic shined through. Her raps were complex, sometimes spit in different accents, and her image, while overtly sexual, reflected her ability to switch quickly between characters, a skill she had honed during her years at LaGuardia.

Minaj's Myspace page turned out to be vital to her career. Fendi, the CEO of Dirty Money Entertainment, found her page and was immediately hooked. Dirty Money Entertainment is a music company that looks to sign and develop underground hip-hop talent in New York City. Through Dirty Money Entertainment, Fendi releases a regular DVD magazine called *Come Up* that features hip-hop artists. Many are from New York and are struggling to make their big break, though the DVD also includes more established voices in mainstream rap. When Fendi heard the tracks posted on Minaj's Myspace page and saw her racy photos, he knew she would be a good fit for *Come Up*. He signed her to his record company and began featuring her on his DVDs.

How Nicki Minaj Got Her Name

When Onika Maraj began working with Fendi, she went by the name Nicki Miraj. Fendi thought the future star deserved a more shocking name, however. When Fendi suggested she become Nicki Minaj, she was not interested; she reportedly thought the name was degrading. Fendi called other rappers to get their opinions and continued to pressure Minaj to change it, and in the end she relented.

Eventually, Fendi and Minaj parted ways, with much animosity. Many of the details of their parting have never surfaced, and Minaj never refers to Fendi by name in interviews. In 2012 a reporter for the *Guardian*, a British newspaper, asked Minaj why she switched from Miraj to Minaj. She replied, "Somebody changed my name. One of the first production deals I signed, the guy wanted my name to be Minaj and I fought him tooth and nail. But he convinced me. I've always hated it."

Quoted in Simon Hattenstone. "Nicki Minaj: 'I Have Bigger Balls than the Boys.'" *Guardian* (Manchester, UK), April 27, 2012. www.guardian.co.uk/music/2012/apr/27/nicki-minaj-bigger-balls-than-the-boys?newsfeed=true.

Lil Wayne Takes Notice

Minaj was featured in numerous volumes of *Come Up*, including the 2006 volume, *The Carter Edition*. This volume spotlighted material from two (unrelated) rap stars, Jay-Z (Shawn Carter) and Lil Wayne (Dwayne Carter). Lil Wayne had never heard of Minaj before the video. After seeing her rap, he contacted Fendi to set up a meeting. Lil Wayne is a very successful rap artist; he has released a number of original studio albums as well as mix tapes. In 2003 he created his own record label, Young Money Entertainment. By 2006, when Lil Wayne spotted Minaj on

Lil Wayne, left, saw Minaj's promise early in her career and helped her record and release her first two mix tapes.

the DVD, he was actively hunting for talent to begin building a competent hip-hop crew for his label.

After meeting Minaj, Lil Wayne immediately wanted to work with her. He saw in Minaj the potential to bring a female voice to hip-hop. He helped steer the first release of her mixtape—a record of rap tracks on which Minaj raps over or samples already recorded songs or melodies—and even appeared on one of her tracks. On July 5, 2007, Minaj released *Playtime Is Over*. Dirty Money Entertainment and Young Money Entertainment released the album together, though all of the tracks were produced by Fendi and another associate from Dirty Money.

After the release of her first mixtape, Minaj moved to Atlanta to be closer to Lil Wayne and Young Money's other artists. She continued to build her career under Lil Wayne's tutelage. In Young Money's studios she created her second mixtape, *Sucka Free*, largely under Lil Wayne's direction. Lil Wayne appeared on eight of the twenty-three tracks, while a few other high-profile rap names, such as Gucci Mane, made cameos on others. The tape, which was released on July 7, 2008, got the attention of several key voices in the hip-hop world. "The young Southside Jamaica, Queens emcee has the lyrical prowess and witty delivery to one day become rap's first lady," wrote a contributor to HipHopRuckus, a hip-hop review site. "Minaj is a serious threat to bubble gum emcees; cat in the hat rhymes will get you embarrassed."[23] Later that year she won best Female Artist of the Year at the Underground Music Awards, an urban music awards event for unsigned artists.

Sharpening Her Skills

In addition to mentoring her and producing her mixtape, Lil Wayne made Minaj a part of his entourage, including her as a special guest on his 2009 *I Am Music* summer tour. She toured the

Minaj gives a live performance in late 2009 after spending the summer on tour with Lil Wayne, who advised her on developing both her music and her image.

Lil Wayne

Lil Wayne, born Dwayne Michael Carter Jr. began his rap career in 1995 when he was just 12 years old, when Cash Money Records partnered him with rapper B.G. to release an album called the *B.G.'z*. A few years later, Lil Wayne teamed up with other young rappers (Juvenile, Young Turk, and B.G.) to create the Hot Boys, a teenage hard-core rap group. The group's second album, *Guerilla Warfare*, made it to the number 1 spot on *Billboard's* List of the Top R&B/Hip-Hop Albums. Four years later, at the age of 16, Lil Wayne released his debut solo album, *Tha Block is Hot*. Finding success in hard-core rap circles, Wayne continued to release solo albums, as well as mix-tapes.

Lil Wayne has discovered and influenced several young rap stars, including Minaj.

In 2003 Wayne founded Young Money Records, an independent record label through which he released his 2004 breakthrough album, *Tha Carter*. His follow-up album, 2005's *Tha Carter II*, was a major success, selling a quarter of a million copies in its first week. After *Tha Carter II*, Wayne continued to release a series of mix-tapes, including *Dedication, Dedication 2,* and *Dedication 3,* that fueled new crossover success for the rapper. Wayne also began to increasingly turn his attention to growing his label's hip-hop posse. By 2009, Lil Wayne had was working with rising stars Drake, Gudda Gudda, Mack Maine, Tyga, and Nicki Minaj, who were all featured in a collaboration album released by Wayne's label called, *We Are Young Money*.

country with Lil Wayne and his Young Money Crew, which also included up-and-coming artist Drake. On tour, Minaj was in awe of how much fans loved Lil Wayne. She was also impressed with his onstage skill and confidence. The experience of touring with Lil Wayne—and working with him in the studio—made Minaj hungry to further develop the full range of her skills.

Lil Wayne was a big influence on Minaj in other ways, too. Her manager at the time advised her to stifle her natural theatricality and play up her sexuality. She says the typical advice she got was not to act "too kooky and weird." She left this manager to work with Lil Wayne, whom she felt helped her tap into her creative spirit. Minaj felt supported by Lil Wayne in a way that no one in hip-hop had supported her before, and she gives him a lot of credit for her success. "I feel like I'm still intertwined with him creatively,"[24] she says.

Minaj appreciated the way Lil Wayne told her the truth about her work. He did not mince words with any of his artists when he thought a lyric did not work or a verse fell flat. He pushed his artists, which in turn made them push themselves. Minaj thought that Lil Wayne was very hard on his artists—but he was equally demanding of himself, which helped her take his feedback seriously and respectfully. "I think he really conditioned my brain to strive for perfection,"[25] she says.

Beam Me Up Scotty

After touring with Lil Wayne's *I Am Music* tour, Minaj was inspired to return to the studio. She focused intently on her lyrics and churned out a new mixtape. In April 2009 she released *Beam Me Up Scotty*. Like *Sucka Free*, this tape featured several guest cameos by prominent rappers, including Gucci Mane, Busta Rhymes, and Gudda Gudda. Though Lil Wayne continued to play a large role in Minaj's career, this album was produced by DJ Holiday, a different Atlanta-based artist and producer.

Shortly after the tape was released, MTV featured *Beam Me Up Scotty* on its website, which gave Minaj mainstream exposure.

Along with MTV's stamp of approval, the tape received numerous positive reviews—several from major media outlets. Kevin McGarry, a music critic for the *New York Times*, thought Minaj had the potential to surpass all the female emcees that preceded her. "Minaj, now the world is ready for you, and the wonders you can do,"[26] he wrote. Another reviewer said that with *Beam Me Up Scotty*, Minaj had earned herself "a reputation for delivering vicious lyrics with a fresh style." The reviewer added that Minaj has "a knack for invoking alternative personalities, adding another layer to her already complex persona."[27]

Cameo Queen

Up to this point, Minaj got a much-appreciated boost when other artists made cameos on her songs. With the increasing popularity of her mixtapes, however, Minaj began to be asked to appear on other artists' songs. In 2008 she was featured in one of Lil Wayne's

Robin Thicke, left, and Minaj perform "Shakin' It for Daddy" at his album release party in 2009.

songs on his much-anticipated album *Dedication 3*. Shortly after this, she received several offers to write hooks and verses for other artists. In 2009 she guested on tracks by Mariah Carey ("Up Out My Face") and Robin Thicke ("Shakin' It for Daddy"), in addition to several tracks by Gucci Mane. Each cameo showcased Minaj's unique style of rapping frantically, changing accents, and throwing around provocatively sexual and violent lyrics.

Minaj quickly became the go-to female rapper to spotlight on songs, filling a clear void in the music industry. In 2010 she appeared on even more tracks, including Trey Songz's "Bottoms Up," Jay Sean's "2012: It Ain't the End," Sean Kingston's "Letting Go," Kanye West's "Monster," Ludacris's "My Chick Bad," Usher's "Lil Freak," and Rihanna's "Raining Men," in addition to a single by Lil Wayne, "Knockout."

Minaj's cameos were distinctive; she was sometimes the most resounding thing about a song. For example, Kanye West's single "Monster" featured some of rap's biggest stars, including Jay-Z and Rick Ross, as well as folk group Bon Iver. Yet many fans and critics thought Minaj outshined them all. Applauding her unique and memorable guest appearances, Brian Hiatt of the *Rolling Stone* noted that Minaj "leaps between styles, voices and personas … rapping with a crazed fury." He added, "It's become her signature trick—as if she's determined to make up for the lack of female voices in hip-hop by providing five or six of them herself."[28]

A Media Magnet

Seven songs that featured Minaj made the *Billboard* Hot 100 list, a weekly list of the one hundred most popular songs in America. In addition, one of Minaj's own songs, her debut single "Your Love," also made the list in 2010. Together these eight songs set a record—Minaj had more singles on the Hot 100 list at the same time than any previous artist in any genre in history. As a result, Minaj won numerous awards. At the 2010 BET Awards, Minaj won Best New Artist as well as Best Female Hip-Hop Artist. At the MTV Video Music Awards the same year, she was nominated for Best New Artist, and she was nominated for a Grammy Award

Minaj gives an acceptance speech at the 2010 BET Awards, at which she was honored as Best New Artist and Best Female Hip-Hop Artist.

for Ludacris's song "My Chick Bad." These achievements were exceptional for any artist, but especially so for one who had not yet released her own album.

"Rapping Is like Poetry"

Nicki Minaj writes all her own lyrics. Early in her career she told *XXL* magazine that if she was heard rapping, the lyrics were her own. Minaj says she will never use lyrics that have been ghostwritten for her (that is, written by someone else), even though many other rappers do so. Minaj thinks lyrics are an extension of a rapper, part and parcel of their art form: "Rapping is like poetry and poetry should be more specific to who's saying it. With singing, I think you can write something and it's more general, it's more universal and anybody can sing it. But with rap, I just find that I gotta write what I rap. If you hear me rapping then I wrote it."

Quoted in Starrene Rhett. "Feature: Nicki Minaj; Climax." *XXL*, November 24, 2008. www.xxlmag.com/features/2008/11/feature-nicki-minajclimax.

Music critics, journalists, and other rappers began heralding Minaj as the revival of the female rap voice. With her voice on many of the hottest songs of 2010, Minaj was heard constantly on the radio. Her mixtapes sold strongly, largely because fans went looking for her name on the Internet after hearing about her somewhere. Mainstream magazines and newspapers began to feature her in interviews and photo shoots.

Minaj also helped build buzz by encouraging, or even spreading, gossip that usually was false. For example, there were rumors that she had a sex tape, was bisexual, and was engaged in a feud with Lil' Kim; all of these rumors were false. Not all of the gossip about Minaj was untrue, however; stories that circulated about her being sued for damaging a rented luxury car were real. Another true fact about Minaj was that the music world was hotly anticipating the release of her first album.

Chapter 3

Crossover Success

With the release of an original studio album, Nicki Minaj carved out a unique identity in hip-hop. The album showcased her freestyle chops and also introduced a poppy, R&B sound that made her a crossover success. In addition, Minaj debuted a ramped up, over-the-top persona that took advantage of her natural theatricality and flair for off-beat fashion and style. This persona added to Minaj's appeal, making her one of the hottest stars in all of music.

Pink Friday

Minaj released her first studio album, *Pink Friday*, on November 23, 2010. She worked on the tracks for over a year, partnering with a number of new producers, including Swizz Beatz and will.i.am (from the Black Eyed Peas). As a result, the production styles of the album go beyond traditional hip-hop and include R&B, pop, and dance sounds. While most songs include at least some trademark Minaj raps, many also feature Minaj singing, and they touch on a wide array of styles and sounds. Minaj describes her style as "hip-hop meets top 40 meets theater."[29]

Minaj also debuted a pumped up, over-the-top persona. Although she had experimented with rapping in different accents and was often photographed in costume or wearing brightly colored wigs, Minaj unleashed the full force of her personality on *Pink Friday*. She introduced alter egos—each with different voices and personalities—and showcased her love of wacky fashion and outrageous costumes and wigs in the album's accompanying

Minaj signs a copy of her first studio album, Pink Friday, *for a fan at an event to promote the release of the record in November 2010.*

music videos and promotional appearances. Before releasing her album Minaj was hesitant to create an image that was too far outside the hip-hop mold of a female emcee. The collaborations she participated in prior to the album's release, however, helped her feel confident in presenting her many sides to the public.

Minaj invited other popular artists to make guest appearances on her album. Young Money label mate and good friend Drake collaborated on the track "Moment 4 Life." Rihanna and

The Meaning of *Pink Friday*

Pink *Friday* was released on November 23, 2010, which fell on the Tuesday before Thanksgiving that year. The Friday after Thanksgiving is a huge shopping day for Americans, traditionally known as "Black Friday" because people flood stores to take advantage of one-day-only pre-Christmas deals and sales. Minaj named her album after this infamous day. Reflecting her love of all things pink, however, she changed the name from "Black" to "Pink." As Minaj put it: "To carry on our great tradition of Black Friday, we are going to switch it up this year … in honor of the Nicki Minaj album and call that day pink Friday and call my album 'Pink Friday.'"

Quoted in Mariel Concepcion. "Nicki Minaj Titles Debut Album 'Pink Friday.'" Video. *Billboard*, August 4, 2010. www.billboard.com/column/viralvideos/nicki-minaj-titles-debut-album-pink-friday-1004107682.story#/column/viralvideos/nicki-minaj-titles-debut-album-pink-friday-1004107682.story.

Natasha Bedingfield, two of Minaj's favorite artists, collaborated on songs, and Kanye West, will.i.am, and Eminem provided cameos as well. Minaj was particularly excited about Eminem's contribution because she sees him as "animated" and "crazy," like herself. She recalls that he suggested that they both take turns adding more lyrics to the song, in order to make it longer. "It was like a true, authentic hip-hop competition," she says. "It was just amazing."[30]

Minaj was proud of her album. With characteristic bravado she asked one interviewer, "Have you ever seen an album this star-studded—from a girl?"[31] In fact, Minaj scheduled her album release the same day that hip-hop stars Jay-Z and Kanye West were also releasing albums, a highly unusual move for a new artist debuting. Minaj's self-confidence, however, did not waver. "I don't care who's dropping on that day," she said. "I'm good."[32]

A Number One Album

Minaj's confidence was well placed. The album debuted at number two on the *Billboard* 200, a list of the hottest albums in the United States. By February 2010 *Pink Friday* had climbed to number one.

Several of the album's singles dominated *Billboard*'s Hot 100 list for more than a year and made stand-out achievements. The single "Your Love" immediately landed in the top twenty of the *Billboard* chart for all songs and charted number one on *Billboard*'s

Minaj attends Billboard's Women in Music Event in December 2011, where she was honored with the magazine's Rising Star Award.

rap chart. Remarkably, Minaj was the first female to have a chart-topping rap hit in seven years, and the only female to do it on a solo single (that is, not as a featured rapper on a male MC's track) since Missy Elliott's "Work It" in 2002. Another song, "Super Bass," became one of the biggest hits of 2010, reaching number three on the *Billboard* Hot 100 list. This made Minaj the first female rapper in more than a decade to have a chart-topping hit on the overall *Billboard* list.

Pink Friday as a whole sold incredibly well, too. Just a month after it debuted, it had sold over 1 million copies and was certified Platinum by the Recording Industry Association of America (RIAA). *Billboard* honored Minaj with its Rising Star Award of 2011.

From Rapper to Song Maker

Despite great success on the charts, reviews of *Pink Friday* were mixed. Though several tracks showcased Minaj's fierce rapping and lyrical skills, *Pink Friday* also featured many songs with a pop or R&B sound. Surprising to some, many of the tracks were led by Minaj's singing, rather than rapping, and many took a straightforward, less weird, and more romantic tone than she had offered in the past.

Mainstream news sources such as the *Washington Post* and *Entertainment Weekly* were excited by Minaj's new sound. Some reviewers thought the best parts of the album were the most theatrical parts. Shirley Halperin of *Cosmopolitan* wrote, "Whether she's appearing as a fairy in the 'Moment 4 Life' video or a space ninja at the end of the postapocalyptic 'Fly,' it's clear that the time she spent as a kid daydreaming about a storybook life was well-spent."[33] Brad Wete of *Entertainment Weekly*, however, thought that the best songs on the album were those in which she allowed her true self to shine through. He wrote that the album was at its best "when she steps off of her throne, vulnerable and helpless on 'Save Me,' uncovering a talent she kept hidden throughout her sidekick days: She sings. Well, if I might add."[34]

Other positive reviews said Minaj acted smartly when she decided to include a pop sound; they thought it was a great way to market herself to a wider audience. The *Washington Post*'s Allison Stewart pointed out that Minaj's move away from foul-mouthed

Drake

Drake's rise to hip-hop royalty is unusual. Unlike many rap stars, Drake's rap lyrics are not informed by years spent on the street or childhood trauma. Rather, Drake spent his childhood as a star of a Canadian teen soap opera, *Degrassi: The Next Generation,* on which he played the wheelchair-bound "Jimmy" for seven seasons of the show.

Drake, left, and Minaj met through their association with Lil Wayne.

Drake is also unusual because he is black and Jewish, a rare combination in the world of rap. His father is African-American, while his mother is Jewish and white. His parents divorced early, so Drake was raised Jewish by his mother, in a Jewish neighborhood in suburban Canada, though he continued to identify strongly with black culture. This made high school difficult for him. He recalls, "I went to a Jewish school, where nobody understood what it was like to be black and Jewish."

Drake began writing and recording raps while starring in *Degrassi.* He released mix-tapes in 2006 and 2007, and one of his singles debuted on BET even though he was an unsigned artist. In 2008, just as *Degrassi* was cancelled, Drake received a call from Lil Wayne inviting him to perform with Wayne's *I Am Music* tour, on which Nicki Minaj was a special guest. Drake's rise to fame followed quickly. He signed with Lil Wayne's Young Money Entertainment in 2009, released his first studio album in 2010, and his songs immediately began appearing on *Billboard's* Hot 100 list.

Both part of the Young Money Crew, Drake and Minaj grew close, bonded by their shared experience of breaking into the rap industry under the tutelage of Lil Wayne, and also by their shared interest in acting.

Quoted in Amos Barshad. "Drake: The Heeb Interview," *Heeb Magazine,* June 18, 2010, http://heebmagazine.com/the-heeb-interview-with-drake-the-worlds-first-black-jewish-hip-hop-star/5386/2.

rapper helped her court superstardom in a way other female rappers have not. Stewart wrote that the album "nibbles at the edges of what female rappers are allowed to do."[35] Minaj acknowledged that she wanted to challenge stereotypes about female rappers and do something completely different. She believed it was important to demonstrate that a female rapper could make an album that did not reference sex or her body. "So I went above and beyond to prove that I could not talk about sex and not talk about my genitalia and still have a successful album."[36]

Some, however, were disappointed that Minaj distanced herself from her street hip-hop style. Some accused her poppy, crossover

Twitter

Nicki Minaj crossed the threshold of 1 million Twitter followers in 2010 before her first album was released. After *Pink Friday* was released, her Twitter follows grew rapidly. By 2012 Minaj had 11 million followers, making her hip-hop's most followed artist.

In April 2012, however, Minaj abruptly suspended her Twitter account after songs from her sophomore album were leaked online, allegedly by the fan website Nicki Daily. After a debate with the website, Minaj tweeted, "Like seriously, its but so much a person can take. Good [expletive] bye," just before ending her account. Since Minaj was such an active user of the website, often responding to fans personally, her fans were deeply disappointed. Nine days after Minaj suspended the account, she returned to Twitter to reactivate her account and announce details about the video for her popular song "Starships." Her follower count was reset during her absence, though her numbers immediately began to climb as soon as she reentered the Twittersphere.

Quoted in *Hollywood Reporter*. "Nicki Minaj Returns to Twitter, Announces 'Starships' Video Premiere." April 25, 2012. www.hollywoodreporter.com/earshot/nicki-minaj-twitter-return-starships-music-video-316603.

album as selling out her true rap roots. Zach Baron of the *Village Voice* was one person who was disappointed that Minaj chose to downplay her talent for hard rap and opt instead for making what he viewed as an uninspired, sugary pop album. He wrote, "*Pink Friday* really is sort of difficult to listen to—the sound of one of rap's world-class personalities having all her clever foibles and idiosyncrasies blasted away and replaced with … platitudes about the power of women? Worse, actually: *badly sung* platitudes about the power of women."[37] Carrie Battan of the *Boston Phoenix* agreed, saying that fans would be "disappointed" by the album, which she called "watered down, sweetened up … Top 40 rap balladry."[38]

Minaj brushed off criticisms like these, however. She claims her artistry has evolved and is proud of the new places she has taken her work. "Before I was a rapper," she says. "Now I'm a song maker."[39]

"Where My Barbies At?"

Regardless of the critics' opinions, Minaj's album was popular with fans, who loved the star's over-the-top, supercharged, fantastical persona. Minaj is passionate about staying connected to her fans. For a long time she continued to maintain her Myspace page, which gave fans immediate access to her new music. As social media has evolved, Minaj has taken full advantage of it: She particularly makes use of Twitter to keep fans updated. She is even known to personally respond to tweets from fans. When preparing to release *Pink Friday*, Minaj stated on Twitter that she would create a Ustream channel to video chat with her fans if she made it to 1 million Twitter followers. When she reached that goal, Minaj chatted for three hours with fans by Ustream and revealed the name of her debut album by calling fans (who had provided their phone numbers on Twitter) directly.

Minaj, like certain other stars, builds rapport with fans by having a personal name for them. While pop star Lady Gaga's fans are known as "Little Monsters," for example, Minaj's fans are called "Barbies." When she first broke onto the rap scene, Minaj referred to her fans as "Bad B------"—a moniker from the lyrics of her early rap songs. As her fans became younger, though, she

Minaj shows off her Barbie pendant, which is the name she's given to her female fans.

grew less comfortable with the name, especially when she realized that some adult fans were bringing their young daughters to see her perform. So she abandoned the name in favor of a more kid-friendly one, naming her fans after a beloved childhood alter ego instead. "Now when I go up there I say, 'Where my Barbies at?'"[40] she explains.

Because she calls her female fans Barbies, or Barbz, calling her male fans Kenz seemed a natural choice. Though Minaj embraces all her fans, she has a special love for the girls. She often signs the breasts of her female fans, and her "Barbies" line up for the honor.

"I think boobs are very empowering," says Minaj. "And signing them is even more empowering. ... I've signed, like, all types of people, and they're so excited to get their boob signed."[41]

This habit, among other behaviors, has sparked rumors that Minaj is bisexual, or dates both men and women. Minaj encouraged these rumors early in her career by spouting lyrics that allude to relationships with women. However, Minaj says she embraces women in an empowering, though not romantic, way. "I'm not gay, but I do love women, and the way I speak about women and treat my female fans is very abnormal," she

As her success has brought her a broader audience, includ-ing younger fans, Minaj has made an effort to trade the provocative image and lyrics of her early career for ones that promote female empowerment.

admits. "I'll reference a girl having a beautiful (behind) or beautiful boobs. I'll kiss my fans, let them touch me. But do I go home with them at night? Hell, no."[42]

Girl Power

Minaj has become a role model for many of her female fans and has enthusiastically embraced this identity. Conscious of her influence on young people, Minaj sometimes tones down her racy persona—which means she has to remember not to curse onstage. She is careful not to clean up her image too much, though. "The girls don't want me to be Miley Cyrus, either,"[43] she explains, referring to pop singer Cyrus's once clean-cut, wholesome image.

One reason Minaj focused less on her sexuality on *Pink Friday* was because she wanted to show her young fans that success as a woman, even in the music industry, does not have to be based on sexuality. She says that she wanted her female fans to realize that sex appeal alone was not enough to get ahead in life. "You've got to have something else to go with that,"[44] she explains.

Viewing herself as a role model has motivated Minaj to preach female empowerment. In place of the sex talk that used to dominate her mixtapes, many of her album songs espouse her version of girl power. She says that she does not feel inferior to males; she wants her female fans to feel the same way and advises them, "You should earn the same thing the male vice president earned. You should demand the same thing."[45]

Chapter 4

Playing Dress Up

An integral part of Nicki Minaj's wild ascension to fame has been her fashion sense. Her fantastical, rainbow-hued, boundary-pushing, chameleon costume creations hold both fans and the media captive. Her ability to transform herself has made her one of today's most watchable stars, as well as a darling of the fashion world.

An Entertainer from Head to Toe

When Minaj broke onto the underground hip-hop scene, her image was explicitly sexual, modeled after rapper Lil' Kim. After she gained more fans and had more freedom to create her image, Minaj began to experiment. She dressed up in costumes, rather than bikinis, for her videos, stage appearances, and photo shoots. Though she continued to play up her sex appeal, she relied less on outfits that were exclusively provocative. In 2009, for example, she dressed as a wide array of characters that included Marilyn Monroe, Mickey Mouse, and Hermione from *Harry Potter*. On the cover of her mix-tape *Beam Me Up Scotty*, she presented herself as Wonder Woman. She also began to dress in a girlish style she would later identify as her alter ego Barbie. *New York* magazine described her look as alternating "between ghetto-fabulous rap moll [the girlfriend of a rap star], pinup, Japanese anime character, and robot."[46]

Minaj has loved clothing, hair, and color—especially pink—since she was a little girl. As a child she loved to dress up and has very specific memories of clothes she loved. For example, she remembers with vivid detail her first American coat: "It was pink

"Give Me My Sweats"

Nicki Minaj shares a love of over-the-top costumes, extravagant wigs, and staggeringly high heels with pop star Lady Gaga. Although Lady Gaga reportedly dresses the same way at home as she does onstage, Minaj does not. Her wigs and costumes are only for show. She prefers a more laid-back look when she is relaxing at home. "I think Gaga is freakin' dope for that," says Minaj of Gaga's insistence on wearing high-fashion around her house. "But I can't be bothered. Give me my sweats. I actually like transforming from completely raggedy to 'Ahhh, I'm ready.' That transformation gives me a high."

Quoted in Shirley Halperin. "Meet the Real Nicki Minaj." *Cosmopolitan*, November 2011. http://web.ebscohost.com/ehost/detail?sid=d249d812-b20a-4fbf-b194-606bd2e7f83 e%40sessionmgr13&vid=2&hid=14&bdata=JmF1dGh0eXBlPWdlbyZnZW9jdXN0aWQ9 9Z2FsaWxlbyZzaXRlPWVob3N0LWxpdmUmc2NvcGU9c2l0ZQ%3d%3d#db=f5h&AN =70249049.

corduroy with fur on the inside of the hood and brown buttons. I was absolutely obsessed with it."[47] Minaj also experimented with her hair as a way to explore different sides of her personality. She hungrily watched musicians and actors, taking note of those whose style pushed boundaries. She particularly loved Cyndi Lauper, a 1980s pop singer who was known for her colorful, creative outfits and brightly dyed hair. "Her style looked like a piece of art to me,"[48] says Minaj.

As she went deeper with her career, Minaj began to realize that her unique sense of fashion and style, and her willingness to constantly change her look, could strategically set her apart from other performers. "I like the idea of doing something that everyone else is not," she says. "That's my thing."[49] Minaj quickly understood that her image could serve as an additional form of entertainment and art. As she says, "Nobody talks about Nicki Minaj without talking about 'the look.' I don't know if that's a good thing or a bad thing, but I like to keep

Minaj has become known for her outrageous costumes and unusual sense of style as well as her music.

people entertained—and I think you should be entertaining from your head to your toes."[50]

Until the release of her first album, Minaj made all her own clothes and was responsible for executing the entirety of her vision for her look. According to John Demsey, group president of Estée Lauder Companies, until recently Minaj was creating outfits by herself in her basement. "Now," he says, "the others want to get their hands on her."[51] Once she burst onto the scene, Minaj began working with a stylist, a hair and makeup team, and a publicist—a whole arsenal of people responsible for bringing to life her vision of what she can look like.

Involved in Every Decision

Unlike many celebrities, Minaj does not employ a full-time stylist, though she frequently works with stylists for special events or photo shoots. She has had a particularly long relationship with stylist Niki Schwan, who has helped bring Minaj's visions for her costumes to life. Schwan has helped Minaj coordinate entire looks, from clothes, to shoes, to makeup, to hair, including any

Minaj walks the red carpet at the American Music Awards in 2010. Although she occasionally works with a stylist, Minaj maintains control of her fashion choices.

props that complete the look (such as a tropical leaf hat, surgical face mask, or stuffed monster doll on a leash, to name a few examples). Stylists like Schwan also direct the look of a video or photo set, including the colors or props used.

Schwan typically pulls together outfits for Minaj by considering clothing from a number of different designers; often she brings five to nine racks of clothing per project, many of which will never be worn. Schwan and her team also personally design and custom-make parts of a costume to most closely match the look Minaj is going for. Minaj also works with some specific costumers, such as Marco Marco of House of Infinite Radness, who designs and creates pieces for her wardrobe. "Nicki is truly able to tap into each project or event and translate how she is feeling and what she wants to portray, almost like a character of herself, each time," says Schwan. "When you have someone as genuine, creative and trend-setting as Nicki … it can be magical."[52]

Though she has an incredible team of people to work with, Minaj is involved at every level of creating her look. "I've always been like that since I was a little girl," she told Matt Lauer during an appearance on *Today*. "I need to be involved. I need to understand it. I need to have everything written out for me. I need to see it. You know, I can't just have people make decisions for me."[53]

Minaj inspires her team to unleash their full range of talents when creating her clothing. She strives for a style that is unique to her, rather than following trends. Says Schwan, "Nicki … has been an amazing client to work with." Schwan believes that one of the reasons Minaj has become a style icon who is adored by her fans is that she does not take herself too seriously. "She incorporates tons of humor into her style and is fearless in her approach, which I think people really admire and appreciate—as an artist, a woman, and a rising icon,"[54] Schwan says.

A Library of Wigs

In addition to working with a stylist, Minaj also has a hair and makeup team. Most important on this team is Minaj's wig maker, Terrence Davidson, who has worked with Minaj since early in her career. Minaj has become well known for her extravagant rainbow-hued hair concoctions. All of her wigs are handmade and

Minaj wears a leopard-spotted wig to match her outfit at the 2011 Grammy Awards. Her collection of more than 500 handmade wigs is an essential part of her wardrobe.

dyed by Davidson. He makes all of Minaj's wigs from real, human hair, rather than synthetic, because synthetic hair cannot be curled. By 2012 Minaj had a collection of more than five hundred wigs, which are stored in a converted room in Davidson's Atlanta home. "Each wig is on a shelf; it's like a library,"[55] he says.

Davidson has created a vast array of wigs: long ones, short ones; wigs with bobs in the front and long manes in the back; bright pink wigs; lime green wigs; wigs that are blonde on one side and blue on the other; and one that begins blonde but fades to a rainbow. One trademark style of wig is a cotton swab–shaped beehive that is often dyed different colors. One of her more famous beehives has leopard spots hand-painted to match her leopard print bodysuit. The beehive shape is one of Davidson's favorites. "That hair—I just love," he says. "It's just so big. The height."[56] Davidson creates each of the wigs at his home, often creating multiples of popular styles. He hand mixes dye himself to make a perfect hue, and creates whatever Minaj needs. For example, Minaj once wanted her hair to match a favorite teal eyeliner. Davidson custom mixed a match.

Davidson has styled hair and wigs for other celebrities, though none of his other clients have ever requested such a range of colors and styles. "With Nicki, I just knew I had to step out of the box," he said. "She has a young fan base who loves the new stuff. She has a fun side. I go into her closet and I see all this color."[57] For special events, Davidson brings ten to fifteen wigs, from which Minaj chooses. As a result, Davidson travels nearly everywhere Minaj does and has become as much a friend as a collaborator. When Minaj was honored at *Billboard*'s Women in Music luncheon, she showed up to the event with an entourage that included Davidson as well as her makeup artist. While other honored artists, such as Taylor Swift, brought a parent or spouse, Minaj brought people who helped her create her image. In her acceptance speech she even thanked Davidson for "creating her."[58]

"Eye Candy"

Nearly every time Minaj steps out in public, she is dressed to entertain and surprise her fans. In part, this is because she believes that being seen in public is just like being onstage. "That's why I play dress up," she explains. "I just want to give people that eye candy."[59] Her looks are so attention-getting that websites such as *Rolling Stone* and MTV keep a slideshow of her best—or wildest—looks.

Minaj has particularly made waves with costumes she has debuted at award shows. At the 2011 MTV Video Music Awards, for example, Minaj wore a Harajuku, Japanese-designer inspired concoction that included a mirrored bustier, knee-high socks, one furry red monster shoe, star-printed tights, and a colorful surgical mask that covered her face. A pink, yellow, and blonde wig was coiled in twirls atop her head, and she carried a stuffed monster doll on a leash. "It's as if a Robot Anime Princess has come to life forcing you to stare,

Minaj turned heads with the Harajuku-inspired costume she wore to the MTV Video Music Awards in 2011. Her look was the object of both praise and ridicule by critics.

trance-like, into her metallic prism peplum while thinking about nothing but dancing ice cream cones and creepy-happy dolls,"[60] wrote reviewer Andi Teran, who called the outfit a masterpiece.

The mask made a particular impression on critics. Chrissy Mahlmeister of MTV Style wrote that Minaj's mask provided "the cutest way possible"[61] to avoid diseases. Liana Maeby was less

Barbie Minaj

In December 2011 Mattel, the toy company that makes Barbie dolls, created a one-of-a-kind Nicki Minaj doll. The doll was dressed as Minaj's Barbie alter ego, and it has a similar look as the image on the cover of *Pink Friday*. The Barbie doll has long, pink hair and bangs and wears towering heels, an elaborate pink bustier, and a sparkly tulle skirt that surrounds the doll like a cloud. Mattel auctioned off the doll for charity; the proceeds of the doll's sale (which fetched over five thousand dollars) benefited Project Angel Food, which provides food for people suffering from HIV and AIDS.

complimentary of the getup, calling it "annoying" and "absurdly over-the-top."[62] The *Huffington Post* agreed and ridiculed the look, saying, "Girlfriend wears an entire Toys 'R Us."[63]

A few months later, Minaj again turned heads when she performed at the 2011 American Music Awards in a robotic suit of armor that had thermometers on her breasts and speakers on her butt. Then, at the 54th Annual Grammy Awards in February 2012, Minaj appeared on the red carpet wearing a bright-red, stylized priest's robe while walking on the arm of a man impersonating the pope. This outfit enraged those who believed she was satirizing the Catholic faith, especially when she proceeded to conduct an exorcism onstage. Bill Donahue of the Catholic League complained that the Recording Academy should not have allowed Minaj to insult Catholicism, and he went so far as to suggest, "Whether Minaj is possessed is surely an open question."[64]

Viva Glam

In addition to criticism, Minaj's outrageous outfits have landed her lucrative endorsement gigs. For years Minaj strategically sought to launch an image that would be compatible with several of her favorite products. A few months before the release of *Pink Friday*,

Minaj, wearing a shirt made of puff balls, attends Carolina Herrera's Spring 2012 fashion show with Vogue magazine editor Anna Wintour, right, in 2011.

for example, Minaj met with John Demsey about whether she could follow Lady Gaga as the next Viva Glam spokesperson for MAC Cosmetics (which is owned by Estée Lauder). MAC felt Minaj was not yet a big enough star to helm the brand, so Demsey proposed a lipstick promotion timed with the release of her album instead.

On the Friday following *Pink Friday*'s release, MAC introduced a "Pink Friday" shade of lipstick online. All three thousand tubes in stock sold within the first fifteen minutes; twenty-seven thousand sold in the following three weeks. The sales were driven entirely by Minaj's ample fan base: Eight out of ten of the buyers had never been to the MAC website before, proving that Minaj was capable of marrying her musical success with her burgeoning fashion brand. Minaj eventually became the Viva Glam spokesperson in 2012.

Over the next year, as soaring album sales proved her star power, Minaj took further steps into the fashion world. In March 2011 Minaj performed for a charity event/fashion show at Christie's, a prominent high-end auction house. By New York City's Fashion Week, February 2011, a week of high-profile fashion shows put on by designers at the forefront of high fashion, Minaj was in high demand. She received personal invitations to attend several of the shows and was photographed wearing her signature mix of outlandish yet fashion-forward outfits. At the Oscar de la Renta show, for example, she wore a leopard-print bodysuit with tights, leopard-print heels, and a fleece stuffed-tiger hat.

At the Carolina Herrera fashion show in New York City, Minaj was a special guest of Anna Wintour, the famous editor of *Vogue* magazine. There Minaj wore a shirt covered in neon puff balls, bright-green fishnet stockings, and a blonde wig of buns piled high on her head. The contrast between Nicki Minaj's style and Wintour's more classy look tickled many in the fashion world and the media, including Minaj. She says that afterward, Wintour sent her an autographed picture of the two of them together because, as Wintour explained, their very dissimilar outfits actually "matched" since they were both wearing orange. When Minaj saw the picture, she exclaimed, "Oh my God, I'm getting this framed!"[65]

A Fashion Forward Icon

Later in the year, Minaj was invited not only to attend but perform at fashion events. In November she performed at a celebration for the launch of Donatella Versace's clothing line for retail clothing company H&M. She was widely photographed with the famous designer and fashion icon, wearing a piece of the collection specially adapted for her. Minaj also wore adaptations of several other pieces during her performance. That evening she wore a lime-green curly wig with a hat made of tropical plants. The spikes of one of the plants actually poked her in the eye

Minaj wears a hat made of tropical plants to the Versace for H&M launch party in November 2011.

while she wore it, requiring her to use special eye medication for a week afterward.

Finally, in 2011 Minaj's iconic style was featured on numerous magazine covers. Perhaps most notable among them was her feature in the fashion and art magazine, W. Minaj was photographed by Italian artist Francesco Vezzoli, who is known for work in film, photographs, and performances that often involve celebrities in unexpected ways. Vezzoli remade Minaj into four different eighteenth-century courtesans, women who attended social functions in a royal court and were sometimes mistresses to important or wealthy men. Minaj wore elaborate powdered wigs and eighteenth-century dresses and posed in sets that mimicked four historic pieces of art. Of the series, Vezzoli said:

> Minaj makes very explicit and challenging use of her beauty and her body, so I thought of comparing her to some of the most famous courtesans in history: the Marquise de Montespan, Comtesse du Barry, Madame de Pompadour, and Madame Rimsky-Korsakov. My idea was to reproduce four iconic portraits of some of the most fascinating females of the past in a series starring an American pop-culture role model. … Luckily enough, the result came out as surreal as it could be.[66]

Minaj has made other gestures as a fashion icon. For example, she helped create a line of OPI nail polishes based on *Pink Friday* and also launched a signature Nicki Minaj fragrance in 2012. One of her goals is to work with a fashion house so she can develop and sell her own clothing line. Minaj wants to design clothes that will reflect her and her fans; she does not like that other rappers create clothing lines that water down their style in order to appeal to the mainstream. She said she wants something that her fans will embrace. "I don't want it to start blending in with the norm," she explains. "I still want the girls to look like they're on the runway and still be fun and still Harajuku."[67]

Although Minaj wants to be associated with fashion, she is clear that she is unwilling to change herself for the fashion world. Determined to stay true to her unique self, Minaj refuses to be stifled by others' opinions of how she should look. Instead, she insists on always presenting herself in a way that is a reflection of her own tastes. "I don't have to do things just to please people," she explains. "The fashion world will have to come to Nicki Minaj, as opposed to Nicki Minaj trying to go to the fashion world."[68]

Chapter 5

The Many Faces of Nicki

Nicki Minaj is unique among performers in that she has several distinct alter ego personalities. Each of these alternate identities has a unique voice, accent, and manner of dress. These personas make appearances on her songs, music videos, and sometimes onstage. Minaj's ability to switch her voice and demeanor mid-verse sets her apart from nearly every other rapper. It is a key part of her fans' fascination with her, too.

Hearing Voices

As a young girl, Minaj created different characters for herself as a way to emotionally escape her family's violence and drama. Later, as an actress, she took the act of changing herself into different characters even deeper. Once she began rapping, she put these talents to good use. From the start, Minaj used British, West Indian, and New York accents in her rap lyrics. By the time she was working on her mixtapes, she was experimenting even further with role-playing. In her early career she rapped as Harajuku Barbie (a Barbie character who dresses in a Japanese-inspired style), black Miley Cyrus, and Nicki Lewinsky. For Minaj, there is no difference between acting and rapping. She says she thinks of performing "as an opportunity to act. ... In each song I'm auditioning a character."[69]

In her guest cameos, Minaj showed off her ability to leap from one distinct voice to another, even within one line of rap. This shapeshifting became a centerpiece of her unusual appeal. Though Minaj

Minaj dons a colorful scarf while appearing as the persona she calls Teresa Nicki while greeting fans at an event in New York City in 2010.

often alluded to distinct personalities behind these voice changes, she did not unveil her full-fledged alter egos until *Pink Friday*.

Each of Minaj's alter egos has a distinct voice, personality, and manner of dress. Roman Zolanski (pronounced Zolan-SKY) is "flamboyant" and "theatrical." she says. There is also Martha, and Barbie. Barbie is short for Harajuku Barbie, and Minaj describes her as "cutesy, innocent."[70] Minaj also makes a distinction between her stage persona, Nicki Minaj, and Onika, the person she is at home. Onika is who she is in real life, whereas Nicki is who she is as a hip-hop artist and businessperson.

Other of Minaj's alter egos appear less often, or are created expressly for particular events. For example, when she appeared on *Lopez Tonight* to promote *Pink Friday*, she invented a new character named Rosa. At a performance at Madison Square Garden, she wrapped a colorful scarf around her head and called

Harajuku

Harajuku is a type of style that originated in Japan. The name refers to a part of Tokyo that is known both for its shopping district as well as a place with unique street fashion. Every Sunday, Japanese youth gather in the Harajuku area dressed in a spectrum of styles, including punk, skater, goth, and hip-hop.

In the United States the term *Harajuku* refers to a style that draws heavily from Japanese cartoon characters (Japanese animation is called anime). It features cotton candy–hued colors—in hair, clothing and makeup—and plays up stereotypical girlishness, usually with short frilly or pleated skirts, knee socks, and hair in pigtails. When Minaj dressed for the 2011 MTV Video Music Awards, she channeled her Harajuku Barbie by decking herself out in a short dress, knee socks, oversized jewelry, and sherbet-colored hair. Several of her accessories were designed by Japanese artist Shojono Tomo.

herself Nicki Teresa. In October 2011 she introduced Female Weezy, an impersonation of her mentor, Lil Wayne. When she becomes Female Weezy, Minaj wears a white tank top, camouflage pants, skater shoes, and a blonde dreadlocked wig. She posted a picture of herself as Female Weezy on her website, and the alter ego was featured alongside the real Weezy, (Lil Wayne) in Birdman's "Y.U. Mad" single.

Minaj's alter egos come to her in an accidental, unplanned way. "I don't really create them," she says. "It's not a conscious decision. I'll just go into the studio and hear a voice. If I keep hearing that same voice, then I'll name the person."[71]

Roman Zolanski

The alter ego Roman Zolanski appeared early in Minaj's guest cameos. On Trey Songz's single "Bottoms Up," for example, Minaj delivers an especially animated verse that she attributes to

Roman. "Roman is very spastic," she explains. "Roman is crazy and Roman is weird and Roman doesn't care."[72] Roman also appears on Kanye West's "Monster" track and has an exchange with another of Minaj's alter egos, the girlish, sweet Barbie.

On *Pink Friday*, Minaj more fully conceptualized Roman and debuted his unique look. Minaj says that Roman is the one who wears some of her most outlandish outfits, such as her outfit for the 2011 Grammy Awards, at which she wore a robotic suit with speakers on her backside. She says that her most outlandish outfits are

Minaj wears a pendant bearing the name of one of her alter egos, Roman, at an event to promote **Pink Friday: Roman Reloaded** *in 2012.*

"definitely not Nicki—it's basically Roman in drag."[73] As for Roman's personality, Minaj thinks of Roman as her gay twin, an angry man who defies others' expectations. "Roman is a crazy boy who lives in me and he says the things that I don't want to say," explains Minaj. "I think he was born out of rage. He was conceived in rage, so he bashes everyone, and he threatens to beat people. He's violent."[74]

Roman's anger offers Minaj a character through which to voice particularly angry, offensive lyrics, and someone to blame should those lyrics be criticized. "He [Roman] wants to be blamed," says Minaj. "I don't want to blame him. I ask him to leave. But he can't. He's here for a reason. People have brought him out. People conjured him up; now he won't leave."[75] One of the more violent, angry songs on *Pink Friday* was "Roman's Revenge," a collaboration between Minaj and Eminem, where both artists rapped as their alter egos (Eminem's is Slim Shady).

Minaj heavily featured Roman on her follow-up album, *Pink Friday: Roman Reloaded*. Roman's name appeared not only in the album's title but in a number of the songs as well, signaling that Minaj's sophomore album would include more hard-core rapping and more street-tough themes than *Pink Friday*.

All in the Family

Some of Minaj's other alter egos are related to Roman. For example, Minaj also impersonates a character called Martha Zolanski, Roman's mother. Martha speaks in an English accent, as does Roman at times. Martha Zolanski is heard at the end of "Roman's Revenge," after Slim Shady and Roman exchange a tirade of angry lyrics. She orders them to wash out their mouths with soap and go to their rooms. Martha made her first appearance in the music video for "Moment 4 Life," in which she appears as a fairy godmother to "King Nicki."

Other of Roman's relatives appear on Minaj's follow-up album, *Roman Reloaded*. One wide-eyed child alter ego is featured on several songs and videos. The childlike voice spews creepy lyrics, speaks with a lisp, and uses childlike body language. This alter ego is rumored to be Roman's little sister, named Loriee Zolanski, though Minaj has not explicitly confirmed this.

Harajuku Barbie

Minaj's Barbie character may be the one she has shown in public for the longest and is the alter ego that inspired her name for her fans. Barbie is the personality that embraces Minaj's love of all things pink. When Minaj is dressed in super-feminine, almost girlish styles, she is most certainly channeling Barbie. As such, Minaj describes this alter ego's personality as "more soft-spoken and sweet. She sounds like a character in a fairy tale."[76]

Over time, Minaj expanded Barbie's name to Harajuku Barbie. Of the name, Minaj said:

> One day I just woke up and put the two words [*Harajuku* and *Barbie*] together because I love the Harajuku culture because the way they dress is the way I am on the inside, like free-spirited, girls-just-wanna-have fun. … That's how I feel and that's what my music is gonna feel like. … So I wanted to merge Harajuku and Barbie because all girls are Barbies. We all want to play dress up. We all want to put on lipstick and be cute and sexy.[77]

For Minaj, the term *Harajuku* reflected the kind of style that she feels best fits her personality. For her, *Harajuku* refers to a Japanese anime–inspired, girlish, candy-colored style of dress and a persona of playful sweetness. In a world where there are many different kinds of "Barbies," making a distinction that she is Harajuku Barbie is a way to set her alter ego apart. When Minaj was featured in *Vibe* magazine in June/July 2010 with a cover photo and photograph spread, she and her stylist worked together to create looks to embody her Harajuku Barbie personality. The cover photo had Minaj dressed in a short pink metallic dress with huge puff sleeves. The front of the dress had a white pinafore (a sleeveless apron worn mainly by small girls), a belt, and a white bow tie at the neck, giving it a distinctly girlish feel. The entire ensemble was very form-fitting and flattering, and Minaj wore thigh-high pink-leather high-heel boots. Accompanying Minaj on the cover were a number of colorful cartoon flowers and two anime characters.

Barbie has shown up on Minaj's mixtapes as well as in her guest cameos, such as in Kanye West's "Monster." She is also on *Pink Friday*

Minaj appears as her Harajuku Barbie character at an event to promote Pink Friday: Roman Reloaded *in London, England, in 2012.*

and can be heard each time Minaj changes her voice to a more inno-cent, girlish sound, and when Minaj sings. In fact, it is Barbie on the album's cover art, which shows Minaj dressed in a glamorous dress, pink hair, and stiletto heels. She is positioned sitting on the floor as a doll would, with her legs digitally altered to appear as long as the infamously impossible proportions of the Mattel Barbie doll.

"The Whole Circus"

As Minaj's popularity has skyrocketed, her alter egos have become the focal point of her career. Late-night talk shows, fan blogs, celebrity magazines, and music journalists love to comment on her alter egos. Music critics point out that Minaj's alter egos dif-ferentiate her from female emcees—and singers in general—who have come before her. Her ability to change her appearance around has helped set her apart in the male-dominated world of hip-hop.

By constantly shifting her look and her persona, Minaj is a dif-ficult target to pigeonhole. Just as crossing over into pop and R&B music proved crucial to Minaj's ascension to mainstream musical success, her alter egos have given her a distinctive element that sets her apart from other pop queens trying to make their mark. David Wallace-Wells of *New York* magazine explains part of the secret of Minaj's success: "She cuts so quickly, in her lyrics and her outfits, from hard-edged supra-masculine to soft-focus and girlie. … The whole circus [of Minaj's alter egos] is dazzling and code-cracking genius, since pop markets run by the same laws as any other: grow or die."[78] Minaj recognizes this and says it is important for her to continually transform herself in order to keep people interested. "You have to always keep people guessing,"[79] she explains.

Not everyone has been thrilled by Minaj's antics or her different alter egos, however. An editorial in *Hyphen* magazine, which cov-ers Asian American culture, takes issue with Minaj's appropriation of Japanese culture, for example. Writer Theresa Celebran Jones questions Minaj's embrace of stereotypical aspects of Japanese culture in the "Your Love" video, which mashes together sev-eral unrelated elements of Japanese culture: In the video, Minaj dresses as a ninja, a samurai, and a geisha, a female entertainer that performs art while wearing elaborate traditional costumes.

By adopting several personas and constantly changing her look, Minaj keeps fans and critics interested in what she will do next.

Celebran Jones writes of the video that it looks "like Japanese culture threw up all over [director] Hype Williams and he decided to shoot a video about it."[80]

Jones also believes Minaj's use of the term *Harajuku Barbie* is based more on the Harajuku fashion Gwen Stefani made popular in the United States rather than the actual fashion in Harajuku, as Minaj says it is. By doing this, Jones wonders if Minaj is appropriating Asian cultural elements without understanding them, and therefore furthering ethnic stereotypes of Asian women and girls.

Religious Nicki

Though the uproar caused by Nicki Minaj's 2012 Grammy performance had many questioning whether she respects religion, Minaj claims to be a believing Christian. In December 2011 she tweeted a Bible verse to her 8 million followers, and a few months later she told the *Guardian* that her heroes are "God. And my mother."

Minaj credits the church for saving her family. After her father attended rehab, when Minaj was grown and out of the house, he and her mother began attending church together. Minaj says that her father became a born-again Christian, and as a result, changed his life.

Quoted in Simon Hattenstone. "Nicki Minaj: I Have Bigger Balls than the Boys." *Guardian* (Manchester, UK), April 27, 2012. www.guardian.co.uk/music/2012/apr/27/nicki-minaj-bigger-balls-than-the-boys.

When Alter Egos Offend

Minaj's 2012 Grammy performance as Roman Zolanski inspired the most virulent criticism of Minaj and her alter egos. Minaj's performance—in which she spoke in tongues, levitated, and acted possessed in the company of backup dancers dressed as altar boys—was the most talked-about performance from that year's show. Many criticized the musician for using over-the-top religious imagery that seemed designed solely for shock value. Maura Judkis of the *Washington Post* wrote that those who watched the performance went from being "confused" to "just plain angry."[81]

Minaj's performance was compared to church-bating pop performances of the past, such as Madonna's "Like a Prayer" and Lady Gaga's "Judas." Chuck Creekmur, the founder of AllHipHop, said that Minaj "was reaching out to the mainstream with this performance, trying to make that full leap into the pop world."[82]

Minaj appears to levitate during her controversial performance at the Grammy Awards in 2012.

Even if religious themes have been exploited in performances before, many were still offended. The Catholic League of America took issue with what they perceived as the perverted way in which Minaj used church symbols in her performance. The league was particularly disturbed by the image of "a scantily clad female dancer stretching backwards while an altar boy knelt between her legs in prayer."[83]

Though Minaj did not apologize for her performance, she said she did not mean to insult anyone, but rather was staying true to the character of Roman. She said the performance reflected her vision of Roman: that though people wanted to exorcise him because he is not normal, he could defy them and rise above.

With her many alter egos, Nicki Minaj has indeed made herself a multifaceted brand, one that is based in an ever-changing persona that can adapt itself to Minaj's creative expression as well as her astute sense of the business side of her game. Minaj understands that her power to channel different personalities, which she honed as a young girl in a trauma-filled home, also has the power to take her career to the next level, allowing her to reinvent herself continually in a music industry that is constantly on the prowl for the next big thing.

Chapter 6

Mogul Minaj

Nicki Minaj considers herself as much a businesswoman as a musical artist. She has set her sights on creating an entire empire, like certain successful male rappers have done. She seeks not just to dominate in music, but to make herself into a brand that can achieve success in a number of businesses, such as the fashion, beauty, and even movie industries. Minaj says her ambition is fueled less by fame or money and more by her childhood dream to offer her family a life without struggle.

Building Her Brand

None of the chart-topping female emcees have managed to maintain an active career for longer than a couple of years. Acknowledging this, Minaj is writing her own formula for her future. Once she began working with Lil Wayne and got serious about her career in rap, she took the helm of her own career, seeing herself as much as a businesswoman as an artist.

Minaj has gone to great lengths to make sure she stays in control of the products she puts out. For example, Minaj turned down early label offers to sign a record deal in order to follow the same strategy that made Lil Wayne wildly successful: She put out consecutive mixtapes, built up a loyal fan base on the Internet, and endeavored to be featured in groundbreaking cameos on other artists' tracks, all before putting out a debut album. When Minaj was ready to record her own original album, she did not automatically sign with Young Money Entertainment, though she had worked with Young Money's founder, Lil Wayne, for over a year. In 2008,

Minaj appears at an event to promote MAC Cosmetics in 2010. She has also served as a pitch person for nail polish, perfume, and soft drinks.

when asked about her debut album, she said, "I have not signed to a major label yet. I'm picky."[84] Minaj did eventually choose to sign with Young Money, but she negotiated a unique deal for herself in which she got complete ownership and rights to her merchandising, endorsements, sponsorships, publishing, and touring. From early in her career, Minaj demonstrated that her eye was as much on the business side of her game as it was on the artistic.

Having secured these rights, Minaj set about making herself into a lucrative brand. Even before *Pink Friday* was released, she began cultivating relationships with corporate sponsors. She first targeted the beauty industry, going after a MAC Cosmetics endorsement deal. In her first two years on the mainstream music scene, Minaj was named the Viva Glam girl for MAC Cosmetics, created a line of OPI nail polishes, released a fragrance, and signed a six-figure endorsement deal with Pepsi. As Laura M. Holson of the *New York Times* said, "Business is booming, thanks in part to Ms. Minaj's behind-the-scenes moves."[85]

Drake + Nicki = Forever?

Though Minaj publicly says she does not date and does not have a significant other, there is much speculation about her relationship with her label mate, rapper Drake. In 2010 Drake and Minaj fueled this speculation when they announced their "marriage" on Twitter. Drake tweeted, "Please refer to @nickiminaj as Mrs. Aubrey Drake Graham and dont stare at her too long. She's finally mine. :)."[1] Nicki also tweeted that Drake was telling the truth. They later told their fans it was just a joke.

Although they are not married, their affection for one another is clear when they appear together in public. A video they did that paired them as a couple also fueled rumors that they are together. Minaj says that although the two of them have a lot in common and are close, they have never dated. "We're like brother and sister, really,"[2] she explains. In 2012 Minaj also denied reports of a romantic relationship with rapper Safaree Samuels whom she considers to be her best friend. And although Drake was rumored to be quietly dating Rihanna, Minaj fans continued to speculate over who was really dating whom.

1. Quoted in Mawuse Ziegbe. "Drake and Nicki Minaj Tweet About Getting Married." MTV, August 27, 2010. www.mtv.com/news/articles/1646718/drake-nicki-minaj-tweet-about-getting-married.jhtml.
2. Quoted in Elaine Welteroth. "Nicki Minaj Crushes the Competition." *Ebony*, (December 2010/January 2011), p. 96.

Minaj claims to be critically aware of each of her moves, thinking several steps ahead about how each deal will earn her what she wants. "I'm smart enough to know what I'm doing all the time," she says. "I'm just adding on to my brand."[86]

Ms. Mogul

From the very beginning of her career, Minaj has been mindful that no female emcee has ever turned her rap deals into an enduring career, though several male rappers have achieved this. *Forbes*, a business magazine, creates an exclusive list each year

Minaj performs with Jay-Z, who has been named by **Forbes** *magazine as one of hip-hop's leading moguls. Minaj wants to be the first woman recognized as a member of that elite group.*

of the wealthiest hip-hop moguls, called the Forbes Five. (In 2012 the top five hip-hop moguls were P. Diddy, Jay-Z, Dr. Dre, Birdman, and 50 Cent). Each year, the list is dominated by men who have made fortunes beyond music by launching lucrative business deals, clothing lines, endorsements, and other kinds of entrepreneurial projects. In her MTV documentary, Minaj asks, "Why isn't there a female rapper-turned-mogul?" She is dissatisfied with this inequality and determined to be the one who rights it. "I want to be the first woman to do it, and I will be."[87]

Minaj says that from the very start she became involved with music as a means to an end. From the time she wrote her first rap verses and sang background vocals in the underground New York rap scene, she dreamed of becoming larger than life. As she explains: "I always looked at [music] like a business, something that I could create an empire out of. So that's why I'm only about to put out my second album and I'm already thinking about this. I had a little conversation with Jay-Z. ... He said, "Congratulations on all your success." And I was like, "Yeah, I'm coming for you. I'm coming for your spot, Mr. Mogul."[88]

Minaj "Bossed Up"

Minaj has a reputation for being very focused on her business. She manages even the smallest details of her image, performances, and projects. She reportedly demands respect and high-quality work from everyone who collaborates with her and rarely goofs around, even in the studio. Joshua Berkman, a Cash Money executive, is impressed by Minaj's determination to learn all aspects of the music industry. "I've never run into that with any other artist,"[89] says Berkman. Kane Beatz, one of the producers Minaj worked with on *Pink Friday: Roman Reloaded*, confirmed this all-business side of Minaj. "Sometimes you go in the studio and people are playing around," he said. "She's not with all that. ... When she's writing, she'll be in the corner. She's not really into the whole showmanship."[90]

Minaj is assertive and professional but says these qualities have opened her eyes to a double standard in the music industry and beyond. She knows that her assertiveness in her business dealings has also earned her a less-than-positive reputation with others. She resents that male artists who have aggressively climbed the ladder to mogul-hood are exalted as "bosses," but women with these qualities and ambitions are more likely to be viewed negatively. "When I am assertive, I'm a b----," she complains. "When a man is assertive, he's a boss. 'He bossed up.' No negative connotation behind 'bossed up,' but lots of negative connotation behind being a b----."[91]

Nonetheless, Minaj plays the role of boss comfortably and confidently. "People either follow suit or they're not around," she told *Vibe* magazine. She says that she is "very black and white when it comes to my business. There's really no gray area. I really don't have a lot of small talk with people I work with. It's pretty much let's get the job done." Minaj explains that she runs a tight ship because she has worked too hard to get where she is to throw it away or mess it up by doing anything to lose the respect of her fans or those with whom she works. "I've done a lot of work. I've put in a lot of blood, sweat, and tears to get here. And I'm not going to allow something minor like loose behavior to ruin my future. I'm just taking care of my image and my business."[92]

Not Boxing Herself In

Expanding her business, Minaj released her second album, *Pink Friday: Roman Reloaded*, on April 3, 2012. She was excited. While her first album was a calculated project, both intended to introduce new fans to Minaj as well as prove to the industry that a female emcee could make a successful chart-topping record, Minaj felt that making this album was more about her own artistic freedom. "I've never had this much fun recording music in my life," she said. "I made a very diverse album."[93]

With *Roman Reloaded*, Minaj felt free to create according to her inspiration, rather than deliver a specific product. She followed her instincts to create an album that both featured a number of songs where she was "spitting" (that is, rapping) as well as tracks that appeal to mainstream audiences.

As the name of the album suggests, Minaj focused this album on her alter ego Roman Zolanski. The first half of twenty-two-track album consists of rap songs, many of which channel Roman and allude to a backstory of Roman being sent to Moscow by his mother to be rehabilitated, a story line Minaj has featured in a video. Many of the lyrics in these songs are expletive-laced and filthy. The second half of the album, however, contains pop songs that feature Minaj's singing.

Minaj holds a copy of her second studio album, **Pink Friday: Roman Reloaded,** *at an event promoting its release in 2012.*

Part Pop, Part Rap

Commercially, the album was another success for Minaj. It debuted at number one on the *Billboard* chart, selling over 250,000 copies its first week. The track "Starships" was the lead single of the album; it immediately hit *Billboard's* Hot 100 list, debuting at number nine, eventually rising to number five, and making the song Minaj's second solo hit to break into the top ten.

Critically, however, the album received mixed reviews, just as her previous album had. Most critics pointed out that the album was exceedingly long and inconsistent, with a rap half and a pop half that had little in common. Adam Fleisher of *XXL* magazine wrote that the album suffered from "not fully being any one thing, as it's unable to balance multiple approaches into one package." He said that the album was "part rap album, part pop album without finding a way to seamlessly balance the two pursuits."[94]

Minaj performs in Birmingham, England, on her tour to promote Pink Friday: Roman Revisited *in 2012. The record was a hit among fans, but it received mixed reviews from critics.*

A *Los Angeles Times* music critic agreed, calling the album "a disjointed, artistically confused release that's not only way too long but also doesn't really ring true as an 'album' at all."[95]

However, some reviewers, such as Tom Ewing of the *Guardian*, believed the mismatched sides of Minaj's album exemplified the star's genius. Ewing described the album as a "triumph" that "makes no attempt to marry its rap and pop impulses. But that doesn't matter—at their best the styles are wedded anyway by a particular frenzy, a sense that Minaj comes with no off switch or lower gear."[96]

Life Without Struggle

Minaj has no plans to slow down in the near future. As she told *Cosmopolitan*, "My whole life is about being Nicki Minaj now. It's a never-ending saga."[97] She is so dedicated to her business plan of building an empire that she leaves no time for a personal life other than spending time with her team and her family. Minaj does not even date because she does not have the time, though celebrity gossip has made much of her relationship with label mate Drake. The most important people in Minaj's life have become the people involved in making her a star. She has employed a number of pre-fame friends and has grown close to her hair and makeup teams, often taking them as her guests to award shows and luncheons.

Minaj's family continues to be very important to her. She is still close to her mother and is invested in her relationship with her youngest brother, who was born while Minaj was in high school. When Minaj began making money from her music, the first thing she did was buy her mother a house. Minaj explains:

> I got her the house I always wanted to live in when I was a kid. ... I finally could breathe this sign of relief. No one could ever really understand, because people equate different types of goals with the moment where you feel really accomplished. Like people think, Oh, well, you broke *Billboard* records or, You signed with Lil Wayne. But to me, the one thing that I had been driving toward was buying my mother a home.[98]

"The Price You Pay"

Despite their tumultuous relationship, Minaj's parents are still together and had another child together, Minaj's youngest brother, in 1998. Her father, Omar Maraj, attended rehab once Minaj was out of the house. He is clean and sober now, and Minaj says, "He doesn't instill fear in people anymore."[1] Nonetheless, his relationship with Minaj remains strained, even though she has forgiven him for causing so much trauma in her childhood. Omar is not happy that Minaj speaks so often about their family's difficult history, but Minaj thinks this is fair and appropriate. "It's the price you pay when you abuse drugs and alcohol."[2] she says.

1. Quoted in Simon Hattenstone. "Nicki Minaj: I Have Bigger Balls than the Boys." *Guardian* (Manchester, UK), April 27, 2012. www.guardian.co.uk/music/2012/apr/27/nicki-minaj-bigger-balls-than-the-boys.
2. Quoted in Brian Hiatt. "The New Queen of Hip-Hop." *Rolling Stone*, December 9, 2010. http://today.msnbc.msn.com/id/40421254/ns/today-entertainment/t/nicki-minaj-new-queen-hip-hop/#.T76JZUob2d9.

Minaj finds happiness in providing for her family. She is often frustrated by the recommendation that she should enjoy her success. "People always tell me that, and it's like they want me to go on an island and go swimming in a Jacuzzi, but that's not what I enjoy," she says. "I enjoy being able to provide for my mother, being able to put my nieces through college. This is stressful, but I wouldn't trade it for the world."[99] For Minaj, the drive to achieve is rooted entirely in the prayers she voiced at the foot of her mother's bed as a child. "Don't get it twisted. It's not about money; it's not about the fame," she says. "It's about I don't have to worry if my little brother is gonna be able to get a new toy for Christmas. It's those little tiny things that really make up the bigger picture. So, my happiness doesn't come from money or fame. My happiness comes from seeing life without struggle."[100]

Notes

Introduction: The Queen of Hip-Hop

1. Quoted in Brian Hiatt. "The New Queen of Hip-Hop." *Rolling Stone*, December 8, 2010, p 78.
2. Mesfin Fekadu. "Nicki Minaj Revives Female Voice in Rap." *Boston Globe*, August 18, 2010. www.boston.com/ae/music/articles/2010/08/18/nicki_minaj_revives_female_voice_in_rap.
3. Quoted in Gerrick D. Kennedy. "Minaj Happy to Be Instrumental in Female Rap Revival." *Vancouver Province*, May 2, 2011.
4. Jody Rosen. "Nicki Minaj: *Pink Friday: Roman Reloaded*." *Rolling Stone*, April 6, 2012. www.rollingstone.com/music/albumreviews/pink-friday-roman-reloaded-20120406#ixzz1tZwFDUsI.
5. David Wallace-Wells. "Shape-Shiftress." *New York*, February 12, 2010. http://nymag.com/fashion/12/spring/nicki-minaj-2012-2.

Chapter 1: Praying for Fame

6. Quoted in MTV. "Nicki Minaj: My Time Now; Minaj Returns Home to Trinidad." Video. www.mtv.com/videos/movies/601325/minaj-returns-home-to-trinidad.jhtml#id=1653117.
7. Quoted in MTV. "Nicki Minaj: My Time Now; Minaj Returns Home to Trinidad."
8. Quoted in MTV. "Nicki Minaj: My Time Now; Minaj Returns Home to Trinidad."
9. Quoted in Judith Newman. "Just Try to Look Away." *Allure*, April 2012, p. 236.
10. Quoted in Hiatt. "The New Queen of Hip-Hop," p. 78.
11. Quoted in MTV. "Nicki Minaj: My Time Now; Minaj Returns Home to Trinidad."

12. Quoted in Jonah Weiner. "Nicki Minaj: Hip Hop's Hottest Sidekick Goes Solo." *Details*, March 2010. www.details.com/celebrities-entertainment/music-and-books/201005/hip-hop-artist-nicki-minaj#ixzz1p1nONwr1.

13. Quoted in Elysa Gardner. "Nicki Minaj Brings Her Theatrical Style to 'Pink Friday.'" *USA Today*, November 23, 2010. www.usatoday.com/life/music/news/2010-11-22-nickiminaj22_CV_N.htm.

14. Quoted in Gardner. "Nicki Minaj Brings Her Theatrical Style to 'Pink Friday.'"

15. Quoted in Judith Newman. "Nicki Minaj; Her *Allure* Photo Shoot." *Allure*, April 2012. www.allure.com/celebrity-trends/cover-shoot/2012/nicki-minaj?slide=2.

16. Quoted in Goodman. "Nicki Minaj, the Rapper with a Crush on Meryl Streep."

17. Quoted in MTV. "Nicki Minaj: My Time Now; Nicki Gets Her Acting On for her 'Right Thru Me' Video." Video. www.mtv.com/videos/movies/601328/nicki-gets-her-acting-on-for-her-right-thru-me-video.jhtml#id=1653117.

18. Quoted in MTV. "Nicki Minaj: My Time Now; Nicki Gets Her Acting On for her 'Right Thru Me' Video."

19. Quoted in Starrene Rhett. "Feature: Nicki Minaj; Climax." *XXL*, November 24, 2008. www.xxlmag.com/features/2008/11/feature-nicki-minajclimax.

20. Quoted in Gavin Godfrey. "Rapper Nicki Minaj: I'll Show You More." CNN, August 26, 2010. www.cnn.com/2010/SHOWBIZ/Music/08/24/nicki.minaj.interview/index.html

21. Quoted in Bang Showbiz. "Nicki Minaj Says Pre-success Work Was Torturous." *Arizona Republic* (Phoenix), August 7, 2011. www.azcentral.com/ent/celeb/articles/2011/08/07/20110807nicki-minajs-torturous-work.html.

22. Quoted in Godfrey. "Rapper Nicki Minaj."

Chapter 2: Collaboration Queen

23 Destro. "Nicki Minaj—Beware Sucka MCs." HipHopRuckus, August 28, 2008. http://hiphopruckus.com/2008/08/on-da-come-up-with-nicki-minaj.html/#.T3IftUobed8.

24. Quoted in *Interview.* "Nicki Minaj on Lil Wayne." April 2010. www.interviewmagazine.com/music/nicki-minaj-on-lil-wayne/#_.
25. Quoted in Clover Hope. "Nicki Minaj: King Me." *Vibe*, February/March 2012, p. 53.
26. Kevin McGarry. "The New Queen Bee: Meet Nicki Minaj." *New York Times Style Magazine*, June 4, 2009. http://tmagazine.blogs.nytimes.com/2009/06/04/the-new-queen-bee-meet-nicki-minaj.
27. Rob Molster. "Minaj Makes Statement with Debut 'Pink Friday.'" *Cavalier Daily* (University of Virginia), December 2, 2010.
28. Quoted in Hiatt. "The New Queen of Hip-Hop," p. 78.

Chapter 3: Crossover Success

29. Quoted in Gardner. "Nicki Minaj Brings Her Theatrical Style to 'Pink Friday.'"
30. Quoted in Elaine Welteroth. "Nicki Minaj Crushes the Competition." *Ebony*, December 2010/ January 2011.
31. Quoted in Gardner. "Nicki Minaj Brings Her Theatrical Style to 'Pink Friday.'"
32. Quoted in Welteroth. "Nicki Minaj Crushes the Competition."
33. Shirley Halperin. "Meet the Real Nicki Minaj." *Cosmopolitan*, November 2011.
34. Brad Wete. "Nicki Minaj's Pink Friday." *EW.com*, November 22, 2010. http://music-mix.ew.com/2010/11/22/nicki-minaj-pink-friday-review .
35. Quoted in Allison Stewart. "Album Review: Nicki Minaj, 'Pink Friday.'" *Click Track* (blog), *Washington Post*, November 23, 2010. http://blog.washingtonpost.com/clicktrack/2010/11/album_review_nicki_minaj_pink.html.
36. Quoted in Hope. "Nicki Minaj," p. 50.
37. Zach Baron and Rich Juzwiak. "Nicki Minaj's *Pink Friday* Debated." *Village Voice*, November 24, 2010. www.villagevoice.com/2010-11-24/music/nicki-minaj-s-pink-friday-debated.

38. Carrie Battan. "Nicki Minaj: Pink Friday." *Boston Phoenix*, November 30, 2010. http://thephoenix.com/Boston/music/112094-nicki-minaj-pink-friday-2010.
39. Quoted in Welteroth. "Nicki Minaj Crushes the Competition."
40. Quoted in Hiatt. "The New Queen of Hip-Hop," p. 79.
41. Quoted in Newman. "Just Try to Look Away," p. 239.
42. Quoted in Gardner. "Nicki Minaj Brings Her Theatrical Style to 'Pink Friday.'"
43. Quoted in Weiner. "Nicki Minaj."
44. Quoted in T. Cole Rachel. "Nicki Minaj." *Interview*. www.interviewmagazine.com/music/nicki-minaj/#_.
45. Quoted in Hiatt. "The New Queen of Hip-Hop," p. 79.

Chapter 4: Playing Dress Up

46. Goodman. "Nicki Minaj, the Rapper with a Crush on Meryl Streep."
47. Quoted in Newman. "Just Try to Look Away," p. 236.
48. Quoted in Kate Sullivan. "Nicki Minaj on Her Wig Collection, Beauty Icons, and More." *Allure*, April 21, 2011. www.allure.com/beauty-trends/blogs/daily-beauty-reporter/2011/04/nicki-minaj-on-her-wig-collection-beauty-icons-and-more.html.
49. Quoted in Larocca. "Cyndi, Barbie, Nicki."
50. Quoted in Gardner. "Nicki Minaj Brings Her Theatrical Style to 'Pink Friday.'"
51. Quoted in Laura M. Holson. "It's Nicki's World." *New York Times*, January 7, 2012. www.nytimes.com/2012/01/08/fashion/nicki-minaj-as-a-rising-style-muse.html?pagewanted=all.
52. Quoted in Miranda Furtado. "Q&A: Nicki Minaj's Stylist, Niki Schwan." *Dose.ca*, May 5, 2011. www.dose.ca/Nicki+Minaj+Stylist+Niki+Schwan/4733889/story.html.
53. Quoted in *Today*. Video. http://video.today.msnbc.msn.com/today/46975774#46975774.
54. Quoted in Furtado. "Q&A."

55. Quoted in Kate Sullivan. "Nicki Minaj's Craziest Wigs." *Allure*. www.allure.com/celebrity-trends/2011/nicki-minaj-wigs#intro.

56. Quoted in Sullivan. "Nicki Minaj's Craziest Wigs."

57. Quoted in Nedra Rhone. "Flair with Hair Boosts Minaj Stylist." *Atlanta Journal-Constitution*, November 28, 2011. www.accessatlanta.com/fashion-style/flair-with-hair-boosts-1243139.html.

58. Quoted in Heather Muir. "Nicki Minaj Has a Beauty Bestie— Would You Want One?" *Allure*, December 13, 2011. www.allure.com/beauty-trends/blogs/daily-beauty-reporter/2011/12/nicki-minaj-has-a-beauty-bestie-would-you-want-one.html.

59. Quoted in Welteroth. "Nicki Minaj Crushes the Competition."

60. Andi Teran. "Full Anatomy of Nicki Minaj's VMA Candy Raver Outfit." MTV Style, August 29, 2011. http://style.mtv.com/2011/08/29/nicki-minaj-raver-vma.

61. Chrissy Mahlmeister. "Minaj Wears Stylish Surgical Mask at 2011 Video Music Awards." MTV Style, August 28, 2011. http://style.mtv.com/2011/08/28/nicki-minaj-surgical-mask-vmas.

62. Liana Maeby. "Questionable Choices: What's Up with Nicki Minaj's VMAs Surgical Mask?" Crushable, August 28, 2011. http://crushable.com/entertainment/questionable-choices-whats-up-with-nicki-minajs-vmas-surgical-mask-846.

63. Ellie Krupnick. "Nicki Minaj VMA 2011 Photos: Girlfriend Wears an Entire Toys 'R Us." *Huffington Post*, August 28, 2011. www.huffingtonpost.com/2011/08/28/nicki-minaj-vma-red-carpet_n_939897.html.

64. Bill Donahue. "Is Minaj Possessed?" Catholic League, March 7, 2012. www.catholicleague.org/is-minaj-possessed.

65. Quoted in Larocca. "Cyndi, Barbie, Nicki."

66. Quoted in *W*. "Agent Provocateurs: Nicki Minaj Transformed by Francesco Vezzoli." November 2011. www.wmagazine.com/artdesign/2011/11/nicki-minaj-transformed-by-francesco-vezzoli?currentPage=2.

67. Quoted in Newman. "Just Try to Look Away," p. 236.

68. Quoted in Hope. "Nicki Minaj," p. 53.

69. Quoted in Weiner. "Nicki Minaj."

70. Quoted in Welteroth. "Nicki Minaj Crushes the Competition."

71. Quoted in Gardner. "Nicki Minaj Brings Her Theatrical Style to 'Pink Friday.'"

72. Quoted in Mawuse Ziegbe. "Trey Songz, Nicki Minaj on Collaborating for 'Bottoms Up.'" MTV, July 14, 2010. www .mtv.com/news/articles/1643637/trey-songz-nicki-minaj-on-collaborating-bottoms-up.jhtml.

73. Quoted in Sullivan. "Nicki Minaj on Her Wig Collection, Beauty Icons, and More."

74. Quoted in MTV. "Nicki Minaj: My Time Now; Nicki Explains, Writes and Spits 'Roman's Revenge.'" Video. www.mtv.com/ videos/movies/601324/nicki-explains-writes-and-spits-romans-revenge.jhtml#id=1653117.

75. Quoted in MTV. "Nicki Minaj: My Time Now; Nicki Explains, Writes and Spits 'Roman's Revenge.'"

76. Quoted in Gardner. "Nicki Minaj Brings Her Theatrical Style to 'Pink Friday.'"

77. Quoted in HipHopStan.com. "Nicki Minaj Explains 'Harajuku Barbie.'" YouTube. www.youtube.com/ watch?v=xkL2r2x6EFg.

78. Wallace-Wells. "Shape-Shiftress."

79. Quoted in Gardner. "Nicki Minaj Brings Her Theatrical Style to 'Pink Friday.'"

80. Theresa Celebran Jones. "Nicki Minaj: The Harajuku Barbie?" *Hyphen*, August 17, 2010. www.hyphenmagazine .com/node/2677.

81. Maura Judkis. "Nicki Minaj's Performance Perplexes Fans." *Click Track* (blog), *Washington Post*, February 13, 2012. www.washingtonpost.com/blogs/click-track/post/nicki-minaj-grammy-performance-perplexes-fans/2012/02/12/ gIQAOGq19Q_blog.html.

82. Quoted in Rob Markman. "Nicki Minaj's Grammy Spectacle Draws Mixed Reaction." MTV, February 13, 2012. www.mtv .com/news/articles/1679117/2012-grammys-nicki-minaj-reactions.jhtml.

83. Quoted in Catholic League. "Is Nicki Minaj Possessed?" February 13, 2012. www.catholicleague.org/is-nicki-minaj-possessed.

Chapter 6: Mogul Minaj

84. Quoted in Rhett. "Feature."
85. Holson. "It's Nicki's World."
86. Quoted in Steven J. Horowitz. "Nicki Minaj Addresses Selling Out by Making Pop Songs." HipHopDX, February 24, 2012. www.hiphopdx.com/index/news/id.18792/title.nicki-minaj-addresses-selling-out-by-making-pop-songs.
87. Quoted in MTV. "Nicki Minaj: My Time Now; What Makes Nicki Minaj Happy?" Video. www.mtv.com/videos/movies/601329/what-makes-nicki-minaj-happy.jhtml#id=1653117.
88. Quoted in Newman. "Just Try to Look Away," p. 236.
89. Quoted in Hope. "Nicki Minaj," p. 53.
90. Quoted in Hope. "Nicki Minaj," p. 53.
91. Quoted in MTV. "Nicki Minaj: My Time Now; Nicki Bosses Up." Video. www.mtv.com/videos/movies/601327/nicki-bosses-up.jhtml#id=1653117.
92. Quoted in Hope. "Nicki Minaj," p. 53.
93. Quoted in Michael Murray. "World Premiere: Listen to Nicki Minaj's New Single 'Starships.'" Ryan Seacrest, February 14, 2012. http://ryanseacrest.com/2012/02/14/world-premiere-listen-to-nicki-minajs-new-single-starships-audio.
94. Adam Fleischer. "Nicki Minaj, *Pink Friday: Roman Reloaded*." *XXL*, April 3, 2012. www.xxlmag.com/reviews/2012/04/nicki-minaj-pink-friday-roman-reloaded.
95. Randall Roberts. "Album Review: Nicki Minaj's 'Pink Friday: Roman Reloaded.'" *Pop & Hiss* (blog), *Los Angeles Times*, April 2, 2012. http://latimesblogs.latimes.com/music_blog/2012/04/album-review-nicki-minaj-pink-friday-roman-reloaded.html.

96. Tom Ewing. "Nicki Minaj: Pink Friday: Roman Reloaded—Review." *Guardian* (Manchester, UK), April 5, 2012. www.guardian.co.uk/music/2012/apr/05/nicki-minaj-pink-friday-review.

97. Quoted in Halperin. "Meet the Real Nicki Minaj."

98. Quoted in Newman. "Just Try to Look Away," p. 238.

99. Quoted in Hiatt. "The New Queen of Hip Hop," p. 79.

100. Quoted in MTV. "Nicki Minaj: My Time Now; What Makes Nicki Minaj Happy?"

1982

Nicki Minaj is born as Onika Tanya Maraj on December 8 to Omar and Carol Maraj in Saint James, Trinidad.

1990

Nicki and her older brother join their parents in Queens after living in the care of their grandmother in Trinidad for several years.

2002

Graduates from LaGuardia High School of Music & Art in New York City.

2004

Begins making appearances on other hip-hop artists' mixtapes.

2006

After signing with New York–based Dirty Money Entertainment, Minaj is featured in several volumes of the DVD magazine the *Come Up*; notably, she appears in volume 11, *The Carter Edition*, which gets her noticed by southern rap superstar Lil Wayne.

2007

Releases her first mixtape, called *Playtime Is Over*, through both Dirty Money Entertainment and Lil Wayne's Young Money Entertainment; Lil Wayne makes a guest cameo on one track.

2008

Releases her second mixtape, *Sucka Free*, through both Dirty Money Entertainment and Young Money Entertainment; Lil Wayne presents all the tracks, as he was more heavily involved in the production; Lil Wayne also features Minaj on a track on his own much-anticipated mixtape, *Dedication 3*, which helps her gain notice in the wider hip-hop community; Minaj is honored at the Underground Music Awards as the Best Female Artist of the Year.

2009

Tours with Lil Wayne as a special guest on his *I Am Music* tour; releases her *Beam Me Up Scotty* mixtape; signs a record deal with Young Money Entertainment in which she maintains rights to all her merchandising, endorsements, touring, and so on; participates in a collaboration album with other Young Money artists, called *We Are Young Money*; is featured on songs by a number of different artists, including Robin Thicke's "Shakin' It for Daddy," Mariah Carey's "Up Out of My Face," and several Gucci Mane songs.

2010

Is featured on numerous artists' tracks, most notably those by Trey Songz ("Bottoms Up"), Jay Sean ("2012: It Ain't the End), Sean Kingston ("Letting Go"), Kanye West ("Monster"), and Rihanna ("Raining Men"); many of the songs Minaj cameos on make it to *Billboard*'s Hot 100 list; with these songs, plus her own debut single, "Your Love," which also makes the Hot 100 list, Minaj breaks a *Billboard* record for the number of hits an artist has on the list; releases her debut studio album, *Pink Friday*; wins Best New Artist, as well as Best Female Hip-Hop Artist, at the BET Awards; is nominated for Best New Artist at the MTV Music Awards.

2011

Appears on *Saturday Night Live* as the musical guest; *Pink Friday* reaches number one on the *Billboard* chart; begins touring as an opening act on Britney Spears's *Femme Fatale* tour; is also featured on Spears's remix of the song "Til the World Ends"; makes numerous appearances at Fashion Week 2011; wins the award for Best Hip Hop Video for the "Starships" video at the 2011 MTV Video Music Awards; is honored as *Billboard*'s 2011 Rising Star; is announced as the next Viva Glam Spokesperson for MAC Cosmetics.

2012

Is nominated for four Grammy Awards, including Best New Artist; her Grammy performance, in character as alter ego Roman Zolanski, is widely panned as too controversial for its religious overtones; releases her sophomore album, *Pink Friday: Roman Reloaded*; it debuts at number one on *Billboard*; makes plans to release a signature fragrance and signs a seven-figure endorsement deal with Pepsi; performs in the half-time show at Super Bowl XLVI with Madonna; is featured on the lead single "Give Me All Your Luvin'" and the song "I Don't Give A" from Madonna's new album, *MDNA*.

For More Information

Books

Ben Westhoff. *Dirty South: OutKast, Lil Wayne, Soulja Boy, and the Southern Rappers Who Reinvented Hip-Hop*. Chicago: Chicago Review, 2011. This book explores southern rap, which has a style that is distinct from grittier New York or West Coast rap. Though Minaj's career began in New York, through her move to Atlanta and her work with Lil Wayne, the party music sound of southern rap heavily influenced Minaj's evolution as an artist.

Periodicals

Shirley Halperin. "Meet the Real Nicki Minaj." *Cosmopolitan*, November 2011.

Brian Hiatt. "The New Queen of Hip-Hop." *Rolling Stone*, December 9, 2010.

Clover Hope. "Nicki Minaj: King Me." *Vibe*, February/March 2012.

Judith Newman. "Just Try to Look Away." *Allure*, April 2012.

Nedra Rhone. "Flair with Hair Boosts Local Stylist." *Atlanta Journal-Constitution*, November 28, 2011.

W. "Agent Provocateurs: Nicki Minaj Transformed by Francesco Vezzoli." November 2011.

David Wallace-Wells. "Shape-Shiftress." *New York*, February 2012.

Elaine Welteroth. "Nicki Minaj Crushes the Competition." *Ebony*, December 2010/January 2011.

Internet Sources

Caryn Ganz. "The Curious Case of Nicki Minaj." *Out*, September 12, 2010. www.out.com/entertainment/music/2010/09/12/curious-case-nicki-minaj?page=0,0.

Simon Hattenstone. "Nicki Minaj: 'I Have Bigger Balls than the Boys.'" *Guardian* (Manchester, UK), April 27, 2012. www .guardian.co.uk/music/2012/apr/27/nicki-minaj-bigger-balls-than-the-boys.

Laura M. Holson, "It's Nicki's World." *New York Times*, January 7, 2012. www.nytimes.com/2012/01/08/fashion/nicki-minaj-as-a-rising-stylemuse.html?pagewanted=all.

New York Times. "A Very Good Year for Nicki Minaj." January 6, 2012. www.nytimes.com/interactive/2012/01/06/fashion/ nicki_minaj_fashion_rise.html?ref=fashion.

Rolling Stone. "Nicki Minaj's Wildest Looks." October 5, 2010. www.rollingstone.com/music/photos/photos-nicki-minajs-best-looks-20101005.

Abby Schreiber. "A Guide to the Many Personalities of Nicki Minaj." *Paper*, April 2012. www.papermag.com/2012/04/a_ guide_to_the_many_personalities_of_nicki_minaj.php.

Andi Teran. "Full Anatomy of Nicki Minaj's VMA Candy Raver Outfit." MTV Style, August 29, 2011. http://style.mtv .com/2011/08/29/nicki-minaj-raver-vma.

Gaby Wilson. "The Best Nicki Minaj Outfits of 2011." MTV Style, December 8, 2011. http://style.mtv.com/2011/12/08/best-nicki-minaj-fashion.

Websites

Cash Money Records (www.cashmoney-records.com). Cash Money is the parent record label of Lil Wayne's Young Money Entertainment. Nicki Minaj's albums are released through Universal Records, Cash Money Records, and Young Money Records.

Nicki Minaj (http://mypinkfriday.com). The official website of Nicki Minaj. It includes Minaj's press releases, links to videos, Nicki Minaj's Twitter feed, a blog that fans can post to, and much more.

Young Money Entertainment (www.weareyoungmoney.com/artist-Pg.jsp?id=4#). This is the website of the record company that signed Nicki Minaj. It includes profiles of Young Money artists, news clips, tour dates, and other promotional information.

Picture Credits

Cover: © SUZAN/PA Photos/ Landov

© AP Images/Chris Pizzello, 15

© AP Images/Jennifer Graylock, 56

© Astrid Stawiarz/Getty Images, 59

© Bill McCay/WireImage/Getty Images, 18

© Brian Ach/Getty Images, 30

© Bryan Bedder/Getty Images, 17

© Christopher Polk/AMA2010/Getty Images for DCP, 48

© D Dipasupil/FilmMagic/Getty Images, 37

© Dan MacMedan/WireImage/Getty Images, 50

© Danny Martindale/Getty Images, 63

© Denise Truscello/WireImage/Getty Images, 26

© Dimitrios Kambouris/WireImage/ Getty Images, 54

© Gregg DeGuire/FilmMagic/Getty Images, 52

© Jamie McCarthy/WireImage for MAC Cosmetics/Getty Images, 70

© Jason LaVeris/FilmMagic/Getty Images, 66

© Jason Sheldon/PA Photos/ Landov, 76

© Jeff Fusco/Getty Images, 75

© John Ricard/Retna Ltd./Corbis, 27

© Kevin Mazur/WireImage/Getty Images, 9, 21, 72

© Kevin Winter/DCNYRE2012/Getty Images for DCP, 47

© Michael Buckner/Getty Images for BET, 43

© Michael Caulfield/WireImage/ Getty Images, 32

© Mike Segar/Reuters/Landov, 19

© NetPics/Alamy, 24

© Ray Tamarra/Getty Images, 28

© Robyn Beck/AFP/Getty Images, 68

© Shareif Ziyadat/FilmMagic/Getty Images, 42

© Todd Williamson/WIreImage/ Getty Images, 39

© ZUMA Press, Inc./Alamy, 61

© ZUMA Wire Service/Alamy, 35

About the Author

Christie Brewer Boyd lives in Cincinnati, Ohio, with her husband and daughter.